A 90-DAY DEVOTIONAL

VISION

WITH

PURPOSE

AND

POWER

DR. MYLES MUNROE

WHITAKER
HOUSE

Vision with Purpose and Power:
A 90-Day Devotional

Munroe Global
P.O. Box N9583
Nassau, Bahamas
www.munroeglobal.com
office@munroeglobal.com

ISBN: 978-1-64123-821-2 • eBook ISBN: 978-1-64123-822-9
Printed in the United States of America
© 2022 by Munroe Group of Companies Ltd.

Whitaker House
1030 Hunt Valley Circle • New Kensington, PA 15068
www.whitakerhouse.com

Library of Congress Control Number: 2021951083

1 2 3 4 5 6 7 8 9 10 11 ᴡ 29 28 27 26 25 24 23 22

CONTENTS

PART THREE: 12 PRINCIPLES FOR FULFILLING PERSONAL VISION: PRINCIPLES 1–6

PART FOUR: 12 PRINCIPLES FOR FULFILLING PERSONAL VISION: PRINCIPLES 7–12

INTRODUCTION

For thirty years, Dr. Myles Munroe counseled and guided thousands of individuals to live lives of personal fulfillment and social and spiritual well-being. The knowledge and experience he gained led him to the conclusion that the central principle of life is *purpose*—and that *vision* is essential for the fulfillment of one's purpose.

As Dr. Munroe shared in his book *The Principles and Power of Vision*, "Vision is the source and hope of life. The greatest gift ever given to mankind is not the gift of sight, but the gift of vision. Sight is a function of the eyes; vision is a function of the heart.... Nothing noble or noteworthy on earth was ever done without vision."

To have vision is to have the faith to believe that the passion in your heart can become a reality. Dr. Munroe explained, "Vision is the key to unlocking the gates of what was and what is, to propelling us into the land of what could be, and has not yet been. Vision sets you free from the limitations of what the eyes can see and allows you to enter into the liberty of what the heart can feel. It is vision that makes the unseen visible and the unknown possible."

Dr. Munroe traveled the world teaching these truths, and he observed, "There are many who have no vision for their lives and wonder how to obtain one. There are others who have a vision but are stuck in the mud of confusion, not knowing what to do next. Then there are those who had a vision but have abandoned it because of discouragement, disillusionment, some measure of failure, or frustration."

From his study of the Scriptures, Dr. Munroe recognized that men and women have unique purposes in God's plan for the world, purposes that are fulfilled by both personal and corporate vision. He encouraged people in countries around the globe to believe in their dreams and to reconnect with their passions. His message was, "Your future is not ahead of you—it lies within you. See beyond your eyes and live for the unseen. Your vision determines your destiny."

As you progress through these ninety devotions, you will discover the "Twelve Principles for Fulfilling Personal Vision." These principles, which are the heart of this book, will further enable you to understand the nature of vision, define vision, capture or recapture personal vision, simplify your vision, and document your vision. If you take these twelve principles to heart, you will be well on your way to achieving your vision. Through the "Action Steps to Fulfilling Vision," you will find practical applications for implementing what you learn so that you can fulfill God's purpose for your life.

Also featured are daily Scripture readings. Since we discover our purpose and vision only in the mind of our Maker, it is essential to read His "Manual," as Dr. Munroe liked to call the Bible, for ourselves in order to clearly see the revelation of His purposes. We must allow God's Word to dwell richly in our hearts so that, as we meditate on and absorb Scripture, it truly becomes a part of our lives.

Whenever we study the Word of God, we should also pray and ask God for wisdom. The Holy Spirit is our Teacher, and we need to ask Him to illuminate the Word and give us insight. May God bless you in your relationship with Him and with those He has placed in your life as you discover *Vision with Purpose and Power* and fulfill your personal vision in this generation.

— Day 1 —

DESTINED TO MAKE A DIFFERENCE

"I know the plans I have for you," declares the LORD, "plans to prosper you and not to harm you, plans to give you hope and a future."   —Jeremiah 29:11

Do you have a sense of personal purpose? Do you know why you were born? Does your purpose give you a passion for living? You may ask me, "Do I really need to have a reason for my existence?" My answer is, "Absolutely!" Life is intended to have meaning; you were not born just for the fun of it. You were meant to be going somewhere, to be headed toward a destination. You can know why you exist, and you can experience a remarkable life in light of that knowledge.

If you ask people, "Why do you exist?" most cannot tell you. They can't explain their purpose in the world. They have no vision for their lives. You were born to achieve something significant. Your life is not a divine experiment but a project of Providence to fulfill a purpose that your generation needs. This purpose is the source of your vision and gives meaning to your life. I want to help you understand the principles of vision and the practical tools and skills necessary to bring your vision into reality.

Think about your life today. What are you using your precious energy on? What are you accomplishing? Do you get up every day with a sense of anticipation and meaning because you know you're doing what you were born to do? Do you feel that your work is a match for your abilities and personality? Or are you pouring your life into your job without feeling fulfilled or having much to show for it? Have you secretly thought you were meant to do something significant in life, but you don't know what it is?

9

I want to encourage you to believe in your daydreams and to reconnect with your passion; your vision awaits your action. Your future is not ahead of you—it lies within you. See beyond your eyes and live for the unseen. Don't let people tell you, "You shouldn't have high expectations." Always expect more than what you have, more than what you are currently doing. Dream big. Somewhere inside you there is always the ability to dream. No matter how challenging it gets, don't give up, because *your vision is the key to fulfilling your life's purpose.*

> Father, You have given us the gift of vision. You have placed unique visions in the hearts of men and women since the beginning of time. Please enable me to understand Your purpose and Your vision for me. In Jesus's name, amen.

Thought: You were born to achieve something significant; you were destined to make a difference in your generation.

Reading: Ephesians 1

— Day 2 —

SEEING WHAT CAN BE

"The word of the LORD came to me, saying, 'Before I formed you in the womb I knew you, before you were born I set you apart.'"   —Jeremiah 1:4–5

No matter who you are or what country you live in, you have a personal purpose, for every human being is born with one. And every person is a leader in his or her own vision, because that person is the only one who can imagine, nurture, and fulfill it.

God has tremendous plans for you that no one else can accomplish! The tragic thing is that too many people live their whole lives without ever recognizing their visions.

Ted Engstrom, the former president of World Vision, told a story that went something like this: A little girl was on a cruise ship, and she and her father were standing on the deck. It was a beautiful, clear day, and the air was crisp and fresh. The little girl, standing on tiptoe, said to her father, "I can't see anything." The father picked her up and put her on his shoulders, so that she was higher than everyone else on the deck and was able to see everything around her. "Daddy!" she exclaimed. "I can see farther than my eyes can look!"

That little girl's statement captures the essence of vision: the ability to see farther than your physical eyes can look—to see not just what is, but also what can be and to make it a reality. One of the greatest gifts God has given humanity is not sight but *vision*. He gave us this gift so we would not have to live only by what we see. Sight is a function of the *eyes*, but vision is a function of the *heart*. You can have sight but not vision.

Throughout history, progress has been made only by people who have "seen" things that were not yet here. *Vision is seeing the future before it comes into being.* It is a mental picture of your destiny.

To paraphrase the Bible, faith is the substance of things you hope to accomplish, the evidence of things you can see even when others cannot. (See Hebrews 11:1 KJV, NKJV.) Vision inspires the depressed and motivates the discouraged. Vision is the foundation of courage and the fuel of persistence. Only by seeing what is not yet here can you bring something new, creative, and exciting into existence.

Thought: Vision allows you to see "farther than your eyes can look."

Reading: Jeremiah 1:4–19

— Day 3 —

VISION IS THE KEY TO YOUR FUTURE

"Where there is no vision, the people perish."
—Proverbs 29:18 (KJV)

The force of vision is one of the most powerful forces in life. In his college economics class, a young man wrote a paper on his vision for overnight mail. The professor took a red pen, gave him a "C," and wrote, "Do not dream of things that cannot happen." The young man left school and started Federal Express. I wonder where the professor is today. Your vision determines your destiny. When you can see what is possible and believe that it can come to pass, it makes you capable of doing the impossible.

At age thirteen, I wrote down my vision for my life. I carried it with me all through junior high and high school. Much of what I'm doing now was on paper when I was a young teenager. Vision makes you persistent. Once you know what you really want and can "see" it, then, no matter what comes against you, you never give up. So, allow me to repeat: *persistence in fulfilling one's life purpose comes from vision.* As long as a person can hold on to their vision, then there is always a chance for them to move out of their present circumstances and toward the fulfillment of their purpose.

I believe with all my heart that when you have no vision, you will simply relive the past with its disappointments and failures. Therefore, vision is the key to your future. Think about what happens to some football teams that are losing the game at halftime. The players go to the locker room and meet with the coach. The coach changes certain game strategies and gives the players a pep talk, telling them what they can accomplish. When they come back

13

out, their whole attitude and perspective seem to have changed, and they win the game.

No matter where you are in life, and regardless of how old or young you are, it can be "halftime" for you. You can reassess your life's strategies and focus on fulfilling your purpose. You can learn to make the necessary adjustments to your life so that you can know how to plan for the future and stop making the same mistakes and decisions that have hindered you in the past.

By the time you finish this devotional, you will be able to see not just what is, but also what can be, so that you can fulfill your personal vision.

~

Thought: As long as a person can hold on to their vision, then there is always a chance for them to move out of their present circumstances and toward the fulfillment of their purpose.

Reading: Hebrews 6:13–20

— DAY 4 —

PURPOSE IS THE SOURCE OF VISION

"The plans of the LORD stand firm forever, the purposes of his heart through all generations."   —Psalm 33:11

The first key to understanding vision is to realize that it always emanates from purpose. Why? God is the Author of vision, and it is His nature to be purposeful in everything He does. Every time He appeared on the scene in human history, it was because He wanted something specific accomplished and was actively working it out through people's lives.

Therefore, God is a God of action based on purpose. Moreover, His purposes are eternal. Psalm 33:11 says, *"The plans of the LORD stand firm forever, the purposes of his heart through all generations."* And Isaiah 14:24 says, *"The LORD Almighty has sworn, 'Surely, as I have planned, so it will be, and as I have purposed, so it will happen.'"* Nothing can get in the way of God's purposes; they always come to pass.

Second, we must understand that God created everything to fulfill a purpose in life. Whether we are talking about a mammal, reptile, plant, star, or person, everything and everyone God created serves a unique purpose. That includes you. You may have been a surprise to your parents, but you were not a surprise to God! He has given you a special purpose to fulfill. The Scriptures say you were chosen in Him before the world began. (See Ephesians 1:4–5.) God planned in advance all that you were born to be and accomplish.

When you understand that purpose is the source of vision, you will learn the secrets to its origin and how it works in your life.

This knowledge will help you take your dream from initial idea all the way to fulfillment.

I am continually positive about life because I know that God created me for a purpose and that He will bring that purpose to pass. Do you believe the same about yourself? Do you know that your life has a purpose? I hope you will become more and more confident of this truth as you seek to understand your personal vision.

> *By the word of the LORD the heavens were made, their starry host by the breath of his mouth. He gathers the waters of the sea into jars; he puts the deep into storehouses. Let all the earth fear the LORD; let all the people of the world revere him. For he spoke, and it came to be; he commanded, and it stood firm.* (Psalm 33:6–9)

Thought: The first key to understanding vision is to realize that it always emanates from purpose.

Reading: Psalm 33

— Day 5 —

YOUR PURPOSE IS ALREADY COMPLETED IN GOD

"I make known the end from the beginning, from ancient times, what is still to come." —Isaiah 46:10

When do you start building a house? Is it when you dig the foundation? Essentially, you begin building whenever the idea for the house is conceived. The finished house is still in the unseen; when other people pass by the property, they don't see it. However, to you, who understands and knows what is going to happen, the house is already finished. Digging the foundation is simply the beginning of bringing your purpose to pass. Therefore, as you dig the foundation, and somebody asks you, "What are you doing?" your answer is very definite. You point to the architect's rendering of the house and say, "I am building this."

Essentially, God has done the same thing with us: He completed us and our purposes before He created us. We must fully realize that not only have our purposes been given to us to manifest in the world, but they have already been finished in eternity. And not only does God establish our ends, but He also gives us glimpses of them through the visions He puts in our hearts. The following verses entirely changed my perspective on the fulfillment of vision:

> *I am God, and there is no other; I am God, and there is none like me. I make known the end from the beginning, from ancient times, what is still to come. I say, "My purpose will stand, and I will do all that I please."* (Isaiah 46:9–10)

In this Scripture, God mentions two things that He does. First, He establishes the end before the beginning. This means that He finishes things first in the spiritual realm, and then He goes back and starts them up in the physical realm. Second, He reveals the end result of something when it is just beginning. God first institutes a purpose, and then He creates someone or something to fulfill that purpose.

Too often, we fail to recognize that when God starts something, He has already completed it in eternity. *"Yet no one can fathom what God has done from beginning to end"* (Ecclesiastes 3:11). We need to remember His order of working: He first tells us what the end of the matter is to be, and then He backs up and begins the process of fulfilling that end—just as a builder first develops an idea and a blueprint and then starts building.

I like this definition: "Vision is foresight with insight based on hindsight." We have insight into God's purposes for us based on what we know God has already accomplished in eternity. We don't know all the details of how our purposes will unfold, but we see their "ends" because God reveals them to us in the visions He gives us. This is why we can be confident that they will come to pass.

Thought: God first institutes a purpose, and then He creates someone or something to fulfill that purpose.

Reading: Isaiah 46:8–13

— Day 6 —

WHAT ARE YOU WIRED FOR?

"The reason I was born and came into the world is to testify to the truth."   —John 18:37

God has given us birth for a purpose. And, as far as He is concerned, that purpose is already finished because He has placed within us the potential for fulfilling it. Your purpose existed before you did. What you were born to do was accomplished by God before you even arrived on the scene, and He ordained your birth to carry it out. God did not create you and then say, "Let me see what I can do with this one." He doesn't create something and then decide what to use it for. He first knows what He wants, and then He assigns someone to accomplish it for Him.

Jesus said, *"The reason I was born and came into the world is to testify to the truth"* (John 18:37). You must have a clear reason for your life, as Jesus did. I know what mine is. I was born to raise up leaders and to train them so they can impact their entire nations for generations to come. That is my reason for living. I was born to inspire and draw out the hidden leader in every human being I meet. I was wired for that. What has God wired you for?

Having a vision, or a dream, is inherent in being human. For true visionaries, the imaginary world of their visions is more real to them than the concrete reality around them. There is a story about when Disney World had just opened and had only one ride. Walt Disney was sitting on a bench on the grounds, seeming to just stare into space. One of his workers, who was manicuring the grass, asked him, "Mr. Disney, what are you doing?" "I'm looking at my mountain," he answered. Walt died before Space Mountain was built, so he never saw it constructed. When Space Mountain was dedicated, the governor and the mayor were present, and Walt's widow was also there. One of the men stood up to introduce her and said, "It's a pity that Mr. Walt Disney is not here today to see this mountain, but we're glad his wife is here." Mrs. Disney walked up to the podium, looked at the crowd, and said, in effect, "I must correct this young man. Walt already saw the mountain. It is you who are just seeing it now."

Always remember that God has a purpose and a vision for your life. And He desires to open your spiritual eyes to see them.

Thought: For true visionaries, the unseen world of their visions is more real to them than the concrete reality around them.

Reading: John 18:28–37

— Day 7 —

BORN TO BE DISTINCT

"I praise you because I am fearfully and wonderfully made; your works are wonderful, I know that full well."
—Psalm 139:14

In economics, the value of something is determined by how rare it is. For example, real pearls are costly because they are found only in a small number of mollusks, and they must be searched for. When you buy a real diamond, it is expensive because no two diamonds in the world are alike. Gold is costly because it is difficult to find. It is the same way with oil; it does not (usually) just spring up in your backyard! You generally have to dig deep to find it.

Similarly, God wants you to be perpetually valuable, so He made you permanently rare. He created you as one of a kind. If you go to a sale at a discount store, you'll notice that many of the dresses, sports coats, or ties on the racks are just alike. You'll see twenty items of clothing with the same pattern and color. They're inexpensive because they were mass-produced. If you want an original dress or suit, however, you have to go to a designer.

You are not like mass-produced clothing; God has not placed you on a sale rack. You are Designer-made. You were born to be distinct. You were designed by God not to blend in but to stand out. Think of the thousands of kinds of flowers in the world. They are all flowers, but each one is unique in its species. Think of a forest. At first glance, the trees all seem to blend together. When you get closer, however, you see that the shape of each tree is unique. Every type of tree has leaves with a distinct design. Why? Uniqueness is part of God's creation.

Individual design is as true of humanity as it is of nature. God doesn't want any one person to get lost in the midst of everyone else. There are over seven and a half billion people on the planet—and not one of them has your fingerprints. We can become complacent about this astonishing truth; it is something we must continually remind ourselves of since it is easy to feel lost in the crowd.

There is no one else like you on earth. Again, God made you that way because He wanted you to be perpetually rare. You are one of a kind, irreplaceable, original. You were born to be distinct and to have a distinct vision.

Thought: You were designed by God not to blend in but to stand out.

Reading: Psalm 139

BORN TO BE KNOWN FOR SOMETHING

*"Wherever the gospel is preached throughout the world, what
she has done will also be told, in memory of her."*
—Mark 14:9

Every human being was created to accomplish something specific that *no one else can accomplish*. It is crucial for you to understand this truth: You were designed to be known for something special. You were meant to do something that will make you unforgettable. You were born to do something that the world will not be able to ignore. It might be a simple act or something more complex; it might be in your hometown or on the world stage. However, it will affect people for the good and help accomplish God's plans for His kingdom.

The Bible is a great Book for recording the stories of people who did little things that the world can't forget. One example is Rahab, the prostitute who risked her life for people she didn't even know. She was born to hide Joshua's spies so that the Israelites could defeat Jericho. (See Joshua 2, 6.) Everyone who reads the Old Testament knows about her act of courage. She chose the people of God over those who opposed them, she married an Israelite, and she became the great-great grandmother of King David and part of the lineage of Jesus Christ. (See Matthew 1:5–6.)

In the New Testament, there is the story of the woman who took an alabaster jar of perfume and anointed Jesus's head with it. She was taking a chance by violating the accepted social code of the day and interrupting a group of men who had gathered for a meal. Yet she decided to pour out her life in gratitude to Jesus, no matter what the consequences. Some of those present severely criticized her because she had "wasted" costly perfume on Jesus when it could have been sold for charitable purposes. Yet Jesus said to them, *"Leave her alone.... Truly I tell you, wherever the gospel is preached throughout the world, what she has done will also be told, in memory of her"* (Mark 14:6, 9).

No matter how small an act may seem, if you put your whole life into it, it won't be forgotten.

Thought: You were meant to do something that will make you unforgettable.

Reading: Joshua 2

— Day 9 —

BORN AT THE RIGHT TIME

"To everything there is a season, a time for every purpose under heaven."   —Ecclesiastes 3:1 (NKJV)

In the book of Ecclesiastes, we read about the revelation of God's purposes to the hearts of humankind. The third chapter begins, *"To everything there is a season, a time for every purpose under heaven"* (Ecclesiastes 3:1 NKJV). God has not only given you a purpose, but He has also determined the time for that purpose to be accomplished. There is *"a time for every purpose."* Whatever you were born to do, God has assigned a season in which it is to be done—and that season is the duration of your life.

Again, God chose when and where you were born for a specific reason. You didn't just show up on earth. Ecclesiastes 3:2 says that there is *"a time to be born."* You were born at the right time to accomplish your vision during your generation. Within this season called life, God has also appointed specific times for portions of your purpose to be accomplished. As you pursue the dream God has given you, He will bring it to fruition during the period of your life when it is meant to be completed. As Ecclesiastes 3:11 says, *"He has made everything beautiful in its time."*

The previous verse states, *"I have seen the burden God has laid on the human race"* (Ecclesiastes 3:10). The word *"burden"* in the Hebrew can actually be translated as "a heavy responsibility" or a "task." It could also be described as a "responsible urge." Every human being comes to earth with a purpose that, in a sense, weighs on him. Whether you are twenty, sixty, or ninety years old, there is a burden within you, a "responsible urge" to carry out all that you were designed to do. It is a cry of the heart—a cry of purpose that says, "I was born to do something that I must fulfill."

Do you sense that cry? Do you feel that you were born to do something with your life? Almost everybody does, even if they have never expressed it. That feeling, longing, or burden comes from God. God has placed a "responsible urge" on your heart because of His purpose for you.

In Ecclesiastes 3:11, we further read, *"He has also set eternity in the human heart."* That is a powerful statement. There is something within you that is being called by eternity. Unless we have turned a deaf ear to it, we wake up each day hearing a call that comes from outside this world. We live in time and space, but time and space are connected to eternity, and God has put something in your heart that calls the unseen into the seen.

The vision God has put in your heart is "a piece of eternity" that He gave you to deliver in time and space—that is, on the earth during your lifetime. What God put into your heart is also what is in His own heart—a piece of eternity.

⌒

Thought: There is something within you that is being called by eternity.

Reading: Ecclesiastes 3:1–13

— Day 10 —
FOR SUCH A TIME AS THIS

*"And who knows but that you have come to your royal position
for such a time as this?"* —Esther 4:14

Esther was a beautiful young Hebrew woman living in exile under the Persian Empire. Through an extraordinary set of circumstances, she became the queen of King Ahasuerus, also known as Xerxes. When she learned of a plot to annihilate the Jews, she discovered that she had been born for a critical purpose: preserving her people. Her uncle told her, in effect, "Perhaps you have become queen for such a time as this."

When Esther accepted her purpose, it became her passion, and she was willing to risk her own life for its fulfillment, saying, *"If I perish, I perish"* (Esther 4:16). Her courage and grace under tremendous pressure influenced the king to agree to a plan to protect the Jews, who were inspired to rally to defend themselves.

Esther was an ordinary woman who was placed in extraordinary circumstances. But she had a clear sense of her purpose and destiny, which produced in her a passion that resulted in a whole nation being saved.

Now consider this: If you do not discover your personal purpose and vision, you will not be able to fulfill your life's assignment. The result is that you will deprive your generation and succeeding generations of your unique and vital contribution to the world.

Suppose Moses had refused to go to Egypt and tell Pharaoh to set the Hebrews free. Consider what the world would be like if, during World War II, Winston Churchill had said, "The survival of Great Britain and the rest of the free world is someone else's problem. I'm going to let the Nazis do whatever they want."

Or suppose Corrie ten Boom had decided that hiding Jews in her home in Nazi-occupied Holland was too risky a proposition.

What if Martin Luther King Jr. had not thought civil rights were worth dying for? And how many people would have died if Mother Teresa had ignored the poor and sick on the streets of Calcutta?

We may never know in our own lifetimes the full impact of our influence and actions, great or small. In light of this truth, developing your vision should not be considered optional for you or for anyone else. The timing of your birth was essential to some need in the world that you're supposed to meet. As you begin to understand the nature and attitudes of true visionaries, you can move toward having the same spirit so that you can make a positive and lasting contribution to your generation.

⌒

Thought: If you do not discover your personal purpose and vision, you will not be able to fulfill your life's assignment.

Reading: Esther 3, 8

— DAY 11 —
YOUR VISION COMPLEMENTS
YOUR PURPOSE

*"The LORD will fulfill his purpose for me; your love, O LORD,
endures forever."* —Psalm 138:8 (NIV84)

I want to clarify the difference between purpose and vision.
Purpose is the intent for which God created you, the reason why
you were born. Purpose is what God has already decided in His
own mind that you're supposed to begin to fulfill. Therefore:

+ *Purpose* is when you know and understand what you were born
  to accomplish.

+ *Vision* is when you can see it in your mind by faith and begin
  to imagine it.

You are not an experiment! When God created you with a
purpose, He also designed you perfectly to be able to fulfill it. This
means He wired you in a specific way so that you would have all
the essential components necessary for fulfilling the vision He
gave you. You never have to worry if you are able to fulfill your life's
purpose. The fact that you were created to complete it means that
you have everything you need to accomplish it. God always gives us
the ability to do whatever He calls us to do.

Vision is a glimpse of your future that God has purposed.
When you are able to see your purpose, your vision comes to life.
As I expressed in a previous devotion, my purpose is to inspire
and draw out the hidden leader in every human being I meet.
However, my vision is to accomplish this through the many facets
of Bahamas Faith Ministries International.

Again, God wouldn't have allowed you to start your life and
your purpose unless they were already completed in eternity. You

were born to manifest something that is already finished. You must realize, however, that your end doesn't look anything like your beginning. This is why you must live by faith, looking forward with expectation for what God has already completed. Otherwise, you will believe only what you see with your physical eyes rather than the vision you see in your heart.

> Father, my life's vision is an exciting look into the future that You have purposed for me. Thank You for assuring me that You have already put the plan in motion in my heart. I am thankful that You will give me the insight to complete it. In Jesus's name, amen.

Thought: God has designed you perfectly to be able to fulfill your purpose.

Reading: 1 Thessalonians 5:23–24

— Day 12 —

VISION IS SPECIFIC

"May he give you the desire of your heart and make all your plans succeed."   —Psalm 20:4

The main thing about vision is that *it is specific*. One of the greatest causes of failure among people who are pursuing their visions is that they don't identify their objective of success. The following may sound simple, but it is very true: people fail because they don't know what they want to succeed in.

Suppose I came to you and said, "Let's meet." You say, "Okay; where?" I reply, "Oh, anywhere." You ask, "Well, *when* do you want to meet?" and I say, "Anytime." What do you think are the chances that we will actually meet? Practically zero. Vision must be specific rather than general or vague.

You need to understand that *vision* is not the same as *mission*. When I ask pastors, "What is your vision?" they generally give me one of the following answers: "My vision is to win my city to Christ." "My vision is to *'preach the gospel to every creature.'*" (See Mark 16:15 KJV.) "Our vision as a church is to know Him and to make Him known." "Our vision is to equip people for the work of the ministry." None of these answers is a *vision* statement. All of them are *mission* statements. Why? They are too general to be vision statements. Vision and mission are related, but they are not the same thing.

A mission is a general statement of purpose that declares the overall idea of what you want to accomplish. It is philosophical and abstract, not practical and concrete. Moreover, it is open-ended, so that you could spend hours, even days, talking about its many aspects and applications. In contrast, *a vision is a very precise statement* that has a specific emphasis and definable boundaries. For example: "Our organization's vision is to reach inner-city youth with Christ's love by establishing a neighborhood youth center."

It is essential that you learn the difference between vision and mission because God is not vague about your life. You were designed to be unique and to fulfill a particular purpose. If you are to carry out your purpose, your vision has to be specific. Remember, your vision—like your fingerprints—is meant to distinguish you from every other person in the world.

⌣

Thought: If you are to carry out your purpose, your vision has to be specific.

Reading: John 21:20–22

HOW DO YOU DISCOVER YOUR VISION?

"Take delight in the Lord, and he will give you the desires of your heart." —Psalm 37:4

Have you discovered your vision yet? The key is this: God's will is as close to you as your most persistent thoughts and deepest desires. Deep inside, you already know your vision.

Psalm 37:4 says, *"Take delight in the Lord, and he will give you the desires of your...."* Desires of your what? *"Your heart"* (verse 4). Wait a minute. Doesn't God give us desires from heaven? Yes, He does. Our desires originated there, but remember that God has placed His desires for you within your heart. He put the plans for your life within you when you were born, and they have never left you. The heart, in this case, means your subconscious mind. God put His plans there because He wants to make sure you find them. Sometimes, His ideas come in multiples. God may put five or six things in your mind that He wants you to do, each one for a different season of your life.

Yet whether He gives you one idea or six ideas, the thoughts of God are consistent. They will be present throughout your life. No matter how old you grow, the same thoughts will keep coming back to you, and the desires will never leave you. This is because the will of God for you never changes. The Bible says, *"God's gifts and his call are irrevocable"* (Romans 11:29). The specifics of your plans may change as your purpose unfolds, but your purpose is permanent. No matter what happens in life, you'll never get away from what God has put in your heart to do.

Vision possesses you; you don't possess it. All the thoughts, ideas, plans, and dreams that remain consistent within you were put there by God. No matter how many times you may temporarily forget about them, they always come back into your mind. Vision is the idea that never leaves you, the dream that won't go away, the passion that won't subside, the "irritating" desire that's so deep, you can't enjoy your current job because you're always thinking about what you wish you were doing. Vision is what you keep seeing, even when you close your eyes. God has placed your vision within your heart.

Thought: God's will for you is as close to you as your most persistent thoughts and deepest desires.

Reading: Psalm 37:3–6

— DAY 14 —
LET GOD GUIDE YOU

"Many are the plans in a person's heart, but it is the LORD's *purpose that prevails."*   —Proverbs 19:21

No person can give you your vision because true vision is not a human invention. It is only God-given. You can go to as many seminars as possible and receive all kinds of wonderful instruction, but no one except God can give you the idea you were born to fulfill.

The poor man, the rich man, the black man, the white man—every person has a dream in his heart. Your vision may already be clear to you, or it may still be buried somewhere deep in your heart, waiting to be discovered. Fulfilling this dream is what gives purpose and meaning to life. In other words, the very substance of life is for you to find God's purpose and fulfill it. Until you do that, you are not really living.

God has a dream and a vision for you that's supposed to carry you right out into eternity because that's what is pulling it. When you die, you're meant to leave this earth not on a pension but on a purpose. You need to make sure you can say at the end of your life, as Jesus did, *"It is finished"* (John 19:30) and not just, "I am retired," for your dream is much bigger than mere retirement.

Vision is what God wants us to contribute in building His kingdom on earth. His purpose was established well before we had any plans for our lives. We were meant to consult God to find out His purposes for us so we can make the right plans. Ecclesiastes 3:14 says, *"I know that everything God does will endure forever; nothing can be added to it and nothing taken from it. God does it so that people will fear [revere] him."*

God wants you to "see" the completion of your vision by knowing that He already planned and established it before you were born. Remember, the fact that you were started is proof that you are already completed because God always finishes before He starts and accomplishes His purposes.

Consequently, at its essence, vision isn't about us—it's about God. Proverbs 19:21 says, "*Many are the plans in a person's heart, but it is the Lord's purpose that prevails.*" True vision is about the desires God imparts to us. It is not our private view of the future; rather, it is the view of our future inspired by God. Therefore, instead of striving to fulfill what God has given you to do, you can rely on Him to finish it as you allow Him to guide you in the specifics of carrying it out.

⌒

Thought: True vision is not a human invention. It's about the desires God imparts to us.

Reading: Philippians 2:13

— Day 15 —

A VITAL CONNECTION WITH GOD

"Abide in Me, and I in you. As the branch cannot bear fruit of itself, unless it abides in the vine, neither can you, unless you abide in Me." —John 15:4 (NKJV)

Many people don't recognize the vision God has placed within them because they don't have a vital connection with Him. This connection needs to be restored before they can see their true purpose. Humankind as a whole lost its relationship with the Creator when man and woman turned their backs on God and tried to pursue their own ways. (See Genesis 3.) God's purpose, however, never changes, and since His purpose is woven into our desires, our own ways are never ultimately satisfying.

God is committed to your purpose, and He provided salvation through Christ to salvage His will and purpose in your life. He said, in effect, "I'm not going to lose what I gave you birth to do. I'm going to save you for your own sake and so I can redeem what I want to accomplish through you." He restores us to Himself so we can do the works He had in mind for us before the world began. *"We are God's handiwork, created in Christ Jesus to do good works, which God prepared in advance for us to do"* (Ephesians 2:10).

We are not saved *by* doing good works but *for the purpose of* doing good works. In other words, we are saved to fulfill our earthly visions. God wants us to accomplish the purposes He's given us to fulfill on earth; that is why He saves us, sanctifies us, and keeps us here for a time.

Once we are restored to God, we receive His Holy Spirit and can see and understand the vision He has placed in our hearts. We learn to discern true vision through our relationship with Him

37

and by reading His Word, because genuine vision is always in alignment with His nature and character. The Bible says, *"Casting down imaginations, and every high thing that exalteth itself against the knowledge of God"* (2 Corinthians 10:5 KJV). This verse is talking about ideas. It continues, *"Bringing into captivity every thought to the obedience of Christ."* Any idea that isn't contrary to the Word of God or to obedience to Christ's wishes for your life is a God idea. God ideas are always in agreement with His will. The Lord would never give you an idea that is contrary to the Bible. That is impossible. Therefore, you are to cast down any ideas that are contrary to His Word. You are to ignore them. If an idea is not in keeping with God's will, set it aside. God has something better in mind for you!

Thought: Genuine vision is always in alignment with God's nature and character.

Reading: John 15

— Day 16 —

HEARING FROM GOD

"Call to Me, and I will answer you, and show you great and mighty things, which you do not know."
—Jeremiah 33:3 (NKJV)

Many people ask me how God speaks to us. They say, "I want to hear from God. Does He speak in an audible voice? Does He come in the night and whisper in my ear? Does He speak through some animal or write on the wall like He did in the Old Testament?" They don't realize that God has been speaking to them since they were born, and He is still speaking to them now. He speaks to them through the thoughts, ideas, and visions they keep having in their minds. If you are unclear about your vision, you can ask God to reveal to you the deepest desires He has placed within you.

At the same time, I have found that some people will wait and wait on God to "tell them what to do" when it has been given to them already. Many religious people, especially Christian people, have been looking for God's will everywhere except within themselves. It's necessary for them to realize that they don't receive their purposes after they are born again; they were already given their purposes when they were physically born. God has saved us because He loves us and because He gave us assignments that He doesn't want to lose. Again, you're not saved for the sole purpose of going to heaven; you're also saved to finish your assignment on earth.

Some nonbelievers will read tarot cards or consult psychics searching for someone to tell them their futures. The sad thing is that some Christians do nearly the equivalent of this when they run from meeting to meeting, asking people to prophesy over them concerning their futures, not understanding that God has given them their visions directly. A true prophet can *confirm* your vision, but he or she will not *give* you your vision. God gives you that directly, and He reveals it to you as you listen to Him and follow Him.

"*I will put my law in their minds and write it on their hearts*" (Jeremiah 31:33). God puts His thoughts within us through the Holy Spirit. What we have to do is listen to what God has given us in our hearts and minds.

Thought: If you are unclear about your vision, you can ask God to reveal to you the deepest desires He has placed within you.

Reading: Jeremiah 29:13

— Day 17 —
SUCCESS FOLLOWS OBEDIENCE

"He made known his ways to Moses, his deeds to the people of Israel."   —Psalm 103:7

God has plans for us, and He wants those plans to be fulfilled. Yet for this to happen, we must follow His direction, His ways. In the first chapter of the book of Joshua, the Lord emphasized the key to fulfilling His plans. Moses had just died, and Joshua was set to take over leadership of the Israelites in order to bring them into the promised land. God said to Joshua, in effect, "Moses is now dead, but you have a big vision; it's your time now to fulfill your purpose. Let's see what you're going to do." The Lord's first advice to Joshua was to be certain *to obey His Word*:

> *Be strong and very courageous. Be careful to obey all the law my servant Moses gave you; do not turn from it to the right or to the left, that you may be successful wherever you go. Keep this Book of the Law always on your lips; meditate on it day and night, so that you may be careful to do everything written in it. Then you will be prosperous and successful* ["have good success" KJV, NKJV]. (Joshua 1:7–8)

In other words, God was saying to Joshua, "You will be successful if you learn and follow My precepts and principles." God guaranteed him success if he would obey the commands that Moses himself had to obey. Please understand that God didn't tell Joshua to literally imitate Moses's *life* but to follow Moses's *principles*, the ones Moses had used in his own work. Likewise, you shouldn't imitate someone else's life. However, you can and should follow the established principles that God has laid out in His Word.

Blessed is the one who does not walk in step with the wicked or stand in the way that sinners take or sit in the company of mockers, but whose delight is in the law of the Lord, and who meditates on his law day and night. That person is like a tree planted by streams of water, which yields its fruit in season and whose leaf does not wither—whatever they do prospers.

(Psalm 1:1–3)

⌒

Thought: For God's plans for us to be fulfilled, we must follow His direction, His ways.

Reading: Deuteronomy 28:1–14

— Day 18 —
UNDERSTANDING THE POTENTIAL OF VISION

"The Lord Almighty has sworn, 'Surely, as I have planned,
so it will be, and as I have purposed, so it will happen.'"
—Isaiah 14:24

Have you grasped the potential of vision? Remember, sight is a function of the eyes, but vision is a function of the heart. Vision is the key to unlocking the gates of what was and what is, to propelling us into the land of what could be. Vision sets us free from the limitations of what the eyes can see and allows us to enter into the liberty of what the heart can feel. It is vision that makes the unseen visible and the unknown possible.

No invention, development, or great feat was ever accomplished without the inspiring power of vision. Civilizations were born and developed through the driving power of visionary leaders. It was vision that inspired Abram to leave the land of Ur and head toward the promised land. Vision inspired the Greeks to produce philosophy and art that still impact the thinking of our world today; vision motivated the great Roman Empire to expand its influence across the known world, and vision inspired the explorers who circumnavigated the globe and ignited the creation and expansion of many nations. Vision gave birth to the thousands of inventions in the last two centuries that have transformed our lives.

Our present world is in desperate need of vision. Even a casual look at the prevailing conditions in our twenty-first century world is enough to produce fear, hopelessness, uncertainty, insecurity, emotional and social trauma, depression, disillusionment, discouragement, and despair. The threat of economic collapse, social disintegration, moral decay, religious conflict, political instability, global health epidemics, ethnic cleansing, and the clash of civilizations demands leadership that can see beyond the now into a preferred future, that has the skill to transfer that vision into reality, and that has the courage to inspire us to go there.

We were all born to do something that leaves nutrients for the seeds of the next generation to take root in and grow. The fact is, we will soon be gone from this earth. Let's make the few years we have here count as we discover and pursue the visions God has placed in our hearts!

~

Thought: It is vision that makes the unseen visible and the unknown possible.

Reading: Ephesians 3:20–21

VISION GIVES YOU PASSION

"Whatever your hand finds to do, do it with all your might."
—Ecclesiastes 9:10

My purpose and vision have become my passion. They wake me up in the morning, and they keep me going when I'm tired. They are an antidote to depression. They cause me to have joy in the midst of great opposition because I know that what God has given me to accomplish cannot be stopped by anyone.

When you discover your true vision, it will give you energy and passion. Finding something you can put your whole self into will fill your life with new hope and purpose. It will give you a reason for living. Ecclesiastes 9:10 says, *"Whatever your hand finds to do, do it with all your might."* The vision in your heart is the spark that will enable you to pursue your dream because unless you do so with all your enthusiasm and strength, it will not happen. I believe the above Scripture expresses a truth that most people miss: you accomplish only what you fight for. If you are merely "interested" in your dream, that dream will never come to pass. However, if you are willing to put all your energy into it, then nobody can stop it from succeeding.

It has been said that there are three kinds of people in the world. First, there are those who never seem to be aware that things are happening around them. Second, there are those who ask, "What just happened?" Third, there are those who *make* things happen.

I have observed firsthand the truth of this statement, paraphrased from John Stuart Mill: *One person with vision is greater than the passive force of ninety-nine people who are merely interested in doing or becoming something.* Most people have an interest in their destinies, but they have no passion or drive to fulfill them. They don't really believe the dreams God has put in their hearts. Or, if they do believe those dreams, they don't do the things that will take them in the direction of fulfilling them. Yet that is what separates the people who make an impact in the world from those who just exist on the planet.

Vision is the primary motivator of human action; therefore, everything we do should be because of the vision God has placed in our hearts. Vision influences the way you conduct your entire life, such as what you spend your time and money on and what your priorities are. Without vision, life has little sense of direction. Time and resources lack purpose.

Vision is the juice of life. It is the prerequisite for passion and the source of persistence. When you have vision, you know how to stay in the race and complete it.

⌒

Thought: One person with vision is greater than the passive force of ninety-nine people who are merely interested in doing or becoming something.

Reading: Colossians 3:23–24

— DAY 20 —

VISION BUILDS UP OTHERS

"Therefore encourage one another and build each other up, just as in fact you are doing."   —1 Thessalonians 5:11

Truevision is unselfish. Its purpose is to bring about God's kingdom on earth and to turn people to Him. *A vision, therefore, should always focus on helping humanity or building up others in some way.*

This means, first of all, that God will never have you pursue your vision at the expense of your family. A beloved friend of mine, who is an older man, went to a conference, and a supposed prophet spoke to him about what God wanted for his life. He came to me afterward and said, "Did you hear what the prophet said?" I said, "Yes." He asked, "What do you think?" I replied, "Well, let's pray over that prophecy. Let's take our time, get counsel, and find God's will on it." The next time I heard from him, he had already set up a plan to fulfill this prophecy. He left his family and went to another country. Was this really God's purpose?

There are instances when members of a family will agree to be apart *for a time* in order to serve a certain purpose. However, this was not the case with this man. When he pursued this prophecy, his wife was frustrated, and his children were confused and angered. He was breaking up his family and causing all kinds of problems and difficulties for them.

If pursuing your vision is causing turmoil in your family, stop and do some serious praying and soul-searching about the situation. Talk with your family members and listen to what they have to say. While you can expect to face some opposition to your vision, and while your family will not always understand or support your dream, pursuing your vision or dream shouldn't destroy the lives of your loved ones. *Vision should always be accompanied by compassion.* You need to be careful and sensitive not to hurt anyone on the way to achieving your goal.

The second thing you should be aware of regarding the unselfish nature of vision is that a true vision will not be all about building a big business just so you can have millions of dollars, an expensive home, a sleek car, and a vacation house on the beach. These things might be goals you have, but they are not true vision—in fact, they are probably selfish ambition. Why? Because they build your kingdom rather than God's kingdom.

Your vision might well involve making a large amount of money. The difference, however, is in your motivation and attitude toward the money. Your perspective on your finances should be God-centered, not self-centered. You need to treat your finances as a resource God has provided to fulfill your vision, not as a tool to fill your life with luxuries.

⌒

Thought: A vision should always focus on helping humanity or building up others in some way.

Reading: Philippians 2:3–4

— DAY 21 —
VISION BRINGS FULFILLMENT

*"That each of them may eat and drink, and find satisfaction
in all their toil—this is the gift of God." —Ecclesiastes 3:13*

Another way you can know that a vision is real is when it is the only thing that gives you true satisfaction. Merely working at a job is disheartening. Going to work is a dismal experience for many people because, day after day, they are doing something they hate. That is not what you were meant for. Ecclesiastes 3:13 says, *"That each of them may eat and drink, and find satisfaction in all their toil—this is the gift of God."* It is God's desire for us to enjoy our work, but this can happen only when we're doing the right work.

Therefore, until you follow God's dream, you will be unfulfilled. Remember, Proverbs 19:21 says, *"Many are the plans in a person's heart, but it is the LORD's purpose that prevails."* No matter what you are busy doing, no matter what you are accomplishing, if it's not what God wants you to do, you won't be completely successful in it. Why? Because true success is not in what you accomplish; it is in doing what God told you to do. That's why people who build big projects or gain great fame can be successful and depressed at the same time.

Going against your purpose may be a personal issue, but it's never a private one. You can mess up others' lives if you aren't supposed to be where you are, or if you are supposed to be somewhere that you refuse to go. Remember the story of Jonah in the Bible? God told him that his purpose was to go to Nineveh to warn the people there to turn to the Lord. Jonah's response was, in effect, "I'm not going!" Instead, he got on a ship headed for Tarshish.

God had purposed that Jonah would go to Nineveh even before the prophet was born. His purpose had already been completed in eternity, and now God was sending him to fulfill it. God didn't want Jonah to be on a ship going to Tarshish when he was meant to go to Nineveh. If you get on any other "ship" besides the one you were meant to get on, you are going to cause others to have problems. In Jonah's case, the ship he got on came in danger of sinking in a terrible storm. Jonah knew God's hand was in the situation, so he told the sailors that the storm would stop if they would throw him overboard. When the sailors did this, the sea became calm, and God provided a great fish to swallow Jonah—protecting him from the sea until he agreed to do what the Lord had called him to do. (See Jonah 1–2.)

I urge you not to board the wrong ship but to remain on course in God's purpose. Maybe you're in the fish's belly right now. You can find your way back to dry land by returning to what God has purposed for you to do.

⌒

Thought: True success is not in what you accomplish; it is in doing what God told you to do.

Reading: Jonah 3

— Day 22 —

YOUR GIFT WILL MAKE A WAY FOR YOU

"A man's gift makes room for him, and brings him before great men." —Proverbs 18:16 (NKJV)

How is the fulfillment of your vision meant to work for you in practical terms? Proverbs 18:16 is a powerful statement that reveals the answer: *"A man's gift makes room for him"* (NKJV). You were designed to be known for your gift. God has put a gift or talent into every person that the world will make room for. It is this gift that will enable you to fulfill your vision. It will make a way for you in life. It is in exercising your gift that you will find real fulfillment, purpose, and contentment in your work.

It is interesting to note that the Bible does not say that a man's *education* makes room for him but that his gift does. Somehow, we have swallowed the idea that education is the key to success. Our families and society have reinforced this idea, but we will have to change our perspective if we are to be truly successful. Education is not the key to success. Don't misunderstand me. I believe in education. However, if education were the only key to success, then everyone who has a PhD should be financially secure and happy.

Education, in itself, doesn't guarantee anything; it is your gift that is the key to your success. The second part of Proverbs 18:16 says, *"A man's gift...brings him before great men"* (NKJV). You don't realize that the gift you're sitting on is loaded. The world won't move over for you just because you're smart. Whenever you exercise your gift, however, the world will not only make room for you, but it will also pay you for it. Anyone—yourself included—who discovers their gift and develops it will become a commodity. If you're a young person in high school or college who is planning your career, don't do what people say will make you wealthy. Do what you were born to do because God's provision for you is there. No matter how big the world is, there's a place for you in it when you discover and manifest your gift.

Michelangelo poured his life into his art. That's why we still remember him five hundred years after he lived. Beethoven and Bach put themselves wholly into their work, and their music lives forever. Alexander Graham Bell believed that sound could be converted into electrical impulses and be transmitted by wire. His passion became a reality, and that is why he is remembered. No matter what God has called you to, your gift will make room for you.

～

Thought: It is in exercising your gift that you will find real fulfillment, purpose, and contentment in your work.

Reading: Romans 12:1–7

—DAY 23—

STIR UP YOUR GIFT

"For this reason I remind you to fan into flame the gift of God, which is in you." —2 Timothy 1:6

God has given each of us a gift, but we have the responsibility to stir it up. The apostle Paul wrote to Timothy, *"For this reason I remind you to fan into flame the gift of God, which is in you"* (2 Timothy 1:6). In other Bible versions, this verse is translated, *"…stir up the gift of God"* (KJV, NKJV). The gift is not something we learn. It is something we need to discover and then stir up. No one else can activate your gift for you. You have to do it yourself.

You stir up your gift by developing, refining, enhancing, and using it. That's where education comes in. Education can't give you your gift, but it can help you develop it so that it can be used to the maximum. Proverbs 17:8 says, *"A gift is as a precious stone in the eyes of him that hath it: whithersoever it turneth, it prospereth"* (KJV). In other words, a gift is like a precious stone to the one who has it, and whenever they stir it up, it turns into prosperity. If you use your gift, it will prosper you. Many people are working only for money. That's an inferior reason to work. We must work for the visions within us.

Moreover, you are not to mimic the gifts of others. You are to stir up your own gift. Unfortunately, many people are jealous of other people's gifts. Let me encourage you not to waste your time on jealousy. Jealousy is a gift robber. It is an energy drain that will take away the passion of life. You should be so busy stirring up your gift that you don't have time to be jealous of anyone else.

I once read an article about Louis Armstrong, the jazz artist, who reportedly applied to go to music school when he was a young man. At his audition, he was given scales to sing, but he could properly sing only the first two notes, and he was told he didn't have what it takes to be a musician. The story said that he cried at first because he had been rejected from the music program, but that he told his friends afterward, "I know there's music in me, and they can't keep it out." He became one of the most successful and beloved jazz musicians who ever lived and sold more records than scores of others who were more talented singers. Now he is forever etched in the history of music.

What made the difference? Louis Armstrong was an original, and he knew it. He wasn't about to waste time feeling sorry for himself. Instead, he put his life and energy into developing the gift he knew he had, and this gift made room for him.

Thought: No one else can activate your gift for you. You have to do it yourself.

Reading: 1 Peter 4:8–11

— Day 24 —

PERSONAL AND CORPORATE VISION

"Just as a body, though one, has many parts, but all its many parts form one body, so it is with Christ."
—1 Corinthians 12:12

Did you know that vision is both personal and corporate? Your personal vision will always be found within a larger, corporate vision. In a corporate vision, God gives a vision to an individual who then shares that vision with like-minded people and transfers it to them. The members of the group, along with the leader, then run with the corporate vision because they find in it a place for their own personal visions to be fulfilled.

Moses was constrained by a vision to deliver the people of Israel out of slavery in Egypt and lead them to the promised land. Joshua was motivated by a vision to possess that land. David was driven by a vision to settle God's people. Nehemiah was possessed by a vision to rebuild the walls of Jerusalem after they were destroyed by Israel's enemies. In every case, the vision was given to an individual who was ultimately responsible for seeing it through, and the individual transferred it to a group.

Many people are needed to fulfill a vision. No great work was ever done by just one person. God will bring together private purposes and visions in order to facilitate corporate success. To better understand this point, read the Bible. Read history. For example, a group of men supported and helped Dr. Martin Luther King Jr. in fulfilling his vision. We all know Dr. King's name, but we hear very little about those other men, even though they were vital for the fulfillment of his purpose. Likewise, we don't know the names of those who helped Moses arbitrate between the people of Israel, but they were an essential support in his purpose of leading the people of God. (See Exodus 18:13–26.)

When a person starts to sense their purpose and gift, if they're not careful, they may interpret it as a call to autonomy and separation. But, again, a sense of personal vision is most often birthed within a broader vision, and it is to be fulfilled in the context of a larger purpose. This is how God weaves personal and corporate vision together. In order to accomplish a corporate purpose, God brings together many people's personal gifts and unique visions. He wants you to bring your time, energy, resources, and creative power to be part of a larger vision to which your vision is connected.

To achieve God's will, we must embrace an attitude of cooperation with those with whom we share corporate vision. Fulfilling your vision requires your being able to submit to others in the larger purpose. It means working with your boss and coworkers in a productive way. It means not trying to undermine the leaders of your group, not letting jealousy get in the way of the vision, and not trying to fulfill the corporate vision all on your own. If we are going to do something for God so that the world will be better off because we were here, we must understand God's ways and work with them rather than against them.

⌒

Thought: God will bring together private purposes and visions in order to facilitate corporate success.

Reading: 1 Corinthians 12

— Day 25 —

DRAWING OUT THE VISION

"The purposes of a man's heart are [like] deep waters, but a man of understanding draws them out."
—Proverbs 20:5 (NIV84)

When we understand the relationship between personal and corporate vision, we will know a chief way in which God fulfills people's dreams. Proverbs 20:5 says, *"The purposes of a man's heart are [like] deep waters, but a man of understanding draws them out"* (NIV84). In other words, everyone has a vision in his heart, but a person of understanding causes that dream, that purpose, that vision to be brought out so it can become reality. A person of understanding can figuratively lower a bucket into the deep well-waters of your soul and begin to draw out what you are dreaming and thinking. They will give life to your desires and thoughts and thereby help make them a reality.

What is the process by which this occurs? After God conveys a vision to a leader, you will—in one way or another—come into contact with this person, who will present the corporate vision; then you will become excited about participating in it because you will see how your private vision finds fulfillment in it. It is essential for you to understand that God brings the corporate vision into your life not to *give* you vision, which He has already given you, but to *stir up* your personal vision. In other words, *you don't receive your vision from other people, but you are enabled to fulfill it through others.* The leader of the corporate vision helps to activate your passions, dreams, gifts, and talents.

It is my desire to stir up your vision. You are a leader in the specific purpose God has given you to accomplish through your gift because no one else but you can fulfill it. I hope my vision of your potential for leadership will excite and motivate you to fulfill the vision in your heart. Are you beginning to dream? Are you able to believe in the possibility of things you never thought possible before? Then you have started to catch the vision for your life.

The corporate vision in which your personal vision will ultimately be fulfilled might be that of a company, a church, a nonprofit organization, or even your own family. That is why, when you hear of something that is related to your vision, you should pay attention to it; it may be that you're supposed to attach yourself to it.

You yourself may be given the corporate vision, such as starting a business or organizing a community project. Yet, remember, none of us is meant to complete our vision on our own. *The joy of God's plan for personal and corporate vision is that nothing we are born to do is to be done by ourselves or for ourselves.* If you and I are part of the same corporate vision, then I need your vision, and you need mine. Therefore, we must stay together and work together. We are not to isolate ourselves in our private successes.

‿

Thought: You don't receive your vision from other people, but you are enabled to fulfill it through others.

Reading: 2 Timothy 1:1–14

— Day 26 —

VISION GENERATES VISION

"Then the LORD replied: 'Write down the revelation and make it plain on tablets so that a herald may run with it.'"
—Habakkuk 2:2

My life's work has been to complete the assignment God gave me. I have not been involved in the work that I'm doing to build a name for myself. Every member of my staff and organization has a part to play in our vision. My part is to stir up their individual dreams, and their part is to stir up mine. When we stir up each other's visions, the divine deposit of destiny starts flowing. Vision generates vision. Dreams always stir up other dreams.

If I ever begin to feel discouraged, I reach out to my friends who also have big dreams. One day, I called my friend Peter Morgan. When he heard my voice, he said, "What's going on?" I said, "I just called to talk to you." He asked, "What's wrong?" "Nothing; just talk to me." "What do you mean?" "Just talk to me. Tell me what you are going to do with your life. Tell me where you are headed. Let me know I'm not alone in pursuing a vision."

You need people around you who believe in dreams that are even bigger than your own so you can keep stirring up your vision. There are too many other people who will tell you to settle down and do nothing. Yet, as we discussed yesterday, a person of understanding can stir up your purposes. A person of understanding can cause your dream to rise from that deep well within you and will help you make real progress toward your vision. You'll begin to believe that no matter where you came from, where you're going is better.

For the revelation awaits an appointed time; it speaks of the end and will not prove false. Though it linger, wait for it; it will certainly come and will not delay. (Habakkuk 2:3)

Today, make some time to follow these actions steps to prepare yourself to begin to implement your life's vision:

ACTION STEPS TO FULFILLING VISION

+ Take half an hour and allow yourself to dream about what you would like to do in life. What ideas and desires do you have? What have you always wanted to do?

+ Think about your primary gifts or talents. How do your dreams and your gifts go together?

+ Have you discovered how your private vision fits into a particular corporate vision? If so, how do they correspond?

+ What "people of understanding" in your life are helping—or can help—to nurture your gift?

+ Write down your ideas, desires, and gifts and read them over every evening for a week. Then ask yourself, "Do these ideas hold true? Are they what I want to do?" If the answer is yes, keep them where you can refer to them as you continue to read *Vision with Purpose and Power*. Watch them form into a specific vision and concrete goals that will move you along toward the completion of your purpose.

Thought: A person of understanding will cause your dream to rise from that deep well within you and will help you make real progress toward your vision.

Reading: Hebrews 10:24–25

VITAL PRINCIPLES FOR FULFILLING YOUR VISION

"Wisdom calls aloud, '...Repent at my rebuke! Then I will pour out my thoughts to you, I will make known to you my teachings.'" —Proverbs 1:20, 23

God has never created a failure. He has designed you, sculpted you, and given you birth to be a success. I have personally seen how God enables people to transform ideas into realities that can be seen in the physical world. The problem is that few people are following the principles that lead to success. Either they don't know the principles or they have never proven them by putting them into practice. A successful person is someone who understands, submits to, and adheres to the principles that will carry them to success.

In this section of devotions, I want to share with you "Twelve Principles for Fulfilling Personal Vision." These principles may be clearly discerned from the Scriptures and the lives of accomplished visionaries, and they are designed to protect, preserve, and guarantee the fulfillment of your dream. Jesus Himself used each one of these principles to be successful in His work of redemption. If you can capture the following, you will see your vision come to pass:

Principle 1: Be Directed by a Clear Vision

Principle 2: Know Your Potential for Fulfilling Vision

Principle 3: Develop a Concrete Plan for Your Vision

Principle 4: Possess the Passion of Vision

Principle 5: Develop the Faith of Vision

Principle 6: Understand the Process of Vision

Principle 7: Set the Priorities of Vision

Principle 8: Recognize People's Influence on Vision

Principle 9: Employ the Provision of Vision

Principle 10: Use Persistence in Achieving the Vision

Principle 11: Be Patient in the Fulfillment of Vision

Principle 12: Stay Connected to the Source of Vision

If you have failed to find or achieve your vision, it is only because you are a success who went off track! You don't have to stay on the sidelines. Your redemption in Christ restores to you the ability to accomplish your vision. When you follow these twelve principles, you will move beyond survival mode; you will be an overcomer and a successful visionary.

∽

Thought: A successful person is someone who understands, submits to, and adheres to the principles that will carry them to success.

Reading: Proverbs 1:20–33

— DAY 28 —

PRINCIPLE 1:
BE DIRECTED BY A CLEAR VISION

"And He [Jesus] said to them, 'Why did you seek Me? Did you not know that I must be about My Father's business?'"
—Luke 2:49 (NKJV)

The first principle for fulfilling personal vision is that *you must have a clear guiding purpose for your life.* Jesus said in Luke 2:49, "I *must be about My Father's business*" (NKJV). There were many other businesses Jesus could have been about, but He identified a specific lifework that was His own and that motivated everything He did, from His youth to His death and resurrection and beyond.

Every effective leader or group of people in history has had that one thing in common: they were directed by a clear vision. Remember that Moses, Joshua, David, and Nehemiah each had a vision that drove them and motivated their actions. Likewise, the first thing God gave to Abraham was a specific vision. He showed him the promised land and said, "That's your vision. You're going to take your offspring there."

I cannot stress enough the need for a guiding vision in life because it is perhaps the single most important key to fulfilling your dream. You personally, as an individual, must have your own guiding life vision. This vision must be *absolutely clear* to you because, otherwise, you will have nothing to aim at, and you will achieve nothing. As I shared earlier, when you know and understand what you were born to accomplish, that is *purpose*. When you can see it in your mind by faith and begin to imagine it, that is *vision*. You cannot contribute to God's greater purposes if you don't know your personal vision. If you have no sense of focus, you will just drift along.

Whether you are young, middle-aged, or older, if you don't have a clear purpose, you are going to be distracted by every other business in the world, because the world is an extremely busy place. You must realize that when you set your mind on what you want to do, all the other business of the world will try to get in the way of it. Having a clear guiding purpose will enable you to stay on track when you are tempted to be distracted by lesser or nonessential things.

Thought: The first principle for fulfilling personal vision is that you must have a clear guiding purpose for your life.

Reading: Genesis 12:1–5

THE WHAT AND THE WHY OF EXISTENCE

"The Holy Spirit said, 'Set apart for me Barnabas and Saul for the work to which I have called them.'" —Acts 13:2

One of my undergraduate degrees is in education, and I had to take a course in biology for a full year as part of my requirements. I really enjoyed that course because it was extremely detailed. We studied the neurological and circulatory systems of the human body, the bone structure, the brain cells, and all the intricacies of how the body works. When I completed the course, I had a sudden thought: "Now that you know *what* the human body is, do you know *why* it is"? Education can give us knowledge, but it can't always give us reasons.

I discovered then that the key to life is not only knowing *what* you are but also *why* you are. *It is more important to know why you were born than to know the fact that you were born.* If you don't know your reason for existence, you will begin to experiment with your life, and that is dangerous. You must capture a meaning for your life, a clear vision for your existence, as described in principle 1 of the "Twelve Principles for Fulfilling Personal Vision." You should know who you are—that is, your origin and purpose in God—as well as your abilities and plans for the future.

Let me ask you some difficult but necessary questions: Do you keep changing your major in college? Do you do one thing for a time and then go on to something else because you are bored or dissatisfied? If so, you lack vision. You were not created to be bored and dissatisfied. For the last thirty years, I have been praying that God would give me an extra day in the week so I can do more work toward my vision. Why? I want to squeeze everything I can out of each day because I have a vision that keeps me passionate. Proverbs 6:10–11 says, *"A little sleep, a little slumber, a little folding of the hands to rest—and poverty will come on you like a bandit and scarcity like an armed man."* Lazy people are visionless people. Bored people are those who haven't yet found their purpose.

You *must* choose where you want to go in life and then be decisive and faithful in getting there. Don't put off the decision or be afraid of it. And don't sell yourself short. While you can't know all the ramifications of your life, which God may reveal to you in eternity, you should have a good idea of the purpose He has given you to accomplish on earth. Without it, all you're doing is existing.

Thought: It is more important to know *why* you were born than to know the fact *that* you were born.

Reading: Acts 13:1–3

— Day 30 —

WHAT IS YOUR TRUE WORK?

"I had not [yet] told anyone what my God had put in my heart to do for Jerusalem."　　　　—Nehemiah 2:12

The Bible is full of illustrations of men and women who were directed by a guiding purpose and a clear vision for their lives. In the Old Testament, Nehemiah is one of those examples. In the years following King Solomon's reign, the city of Jerusalem was attacked by the Babylonian army; its walls were torn down, and Solomon's temple was destroyed. Tens of thousands of Jews were taken to Babylon in captivity. Years later, Nehemiah was an Israelite still living in exile. Through his story, we have a perfect illustration of the difference between simply having a job and having a clear vision for your life.

The Persians had subsequently defeated the Babylonians, and Nehemiah had an important position in the Persian court as cupbearer to King Artaxerxes. (See Nehemiah 1:11.) This position may have included both serving wine to the king and his royal guests and tasting the king's wine to make sure it wasn't poisoned. Yet being a cupbearer meant much more than this. Nehemiah was in a top position in the king's court and was a highly regarded, trusted, and influential advisor to the king.*

I like to think of Nehemiah's cupbearer job as his preliminary occupation, or his "pre-occupation," because he was born to fulfill another, much more important role. This role was ignited by a report on the condition of the city of Jerusalem: Nehemiah heard that *"the wall of Jerusalem [was] broken down, and its gates [had] been burned with fire"* (Nehemiah 1:3). This news filled him with grief, and he *"sat down and wept. For some days* [he] *mourned and fasted and prayed before the God of heaven"* (Nehemiah 1:4).

Your true work is what you were born to do. Your job is what you do only until you are ready to fulfill your vision. During a time of prayer and fasting, Nehemiah received a vision to rebuild the wall: *"I had not* [yet] *told anyone what my God had put in my heart to do for Jerusalem"* (Nehemiah 2:12). He went to God in prayer, and God told him to go back and reconstruct the wall of Jerusalem. This became the compelling vision of Nehemiah's life.

Nehemiah 2:1 reads, *"When wine was brought for him, I took the wine and gave it to the king. I had not been sad in his presence before."* The implication here is that Nehemiah was doing fine on his job until he heard about the wall. His desire to accomplish his life's work then began to interfere with his job. He was employed by the king, but his yearning to rebuild the wall began to wear on him, and it showed. The king said to him, *"Why does your face look so sad when you are not ill? This can be nothing but sadness of heart"* (Nehemiah 2:2).

When God gives you a vision and confirms it, nothing can stop it. If He tells you to build, start, invest, create, or manufacture something, then it will bother you deep inside; you won't be satisfied until you do it.

⌒

Thought: Your job is what you do only until you are ready to fulfill your vision.

Reading: Nehemiah 1

---

*See R. Laird Harris, "Nehemiah," in *The New International Dictionary of the Bible*, J. D. Douglas and Merrill C. Tenney, eds. (Grand Rapids, MI: Zondervan Publishing House, 1987), 699; and *The Wesley Bible: A Personal Study Bible for Holy Living*, Albert F. Harper, gen. ed. (Nashville: Thomas Nelson Publishers, 1990), 669.

— DAY 31 —
WHAT DO YOU WANT?

*"Let [the king] send me to the city in Judah where my
ancestors are buried so that I can rebuild it."*
—Nehemiah 2:5

When King Artaxerxes saw his cupbearer's sadness, he asked
him one of the most significant questions anyone can ask a person:
"What is it you want?" (Nehemiah 2:4). What is equally significant
is that Nehemiah was able to answer it specifically. He said, *"Let
[the king] send me to the city in Judah where my ancestors are buried
so that I can rebuild it"* (verse 5). Nehemiah knew his clear guiding
vision, and his plan was so specific that he was able to give the king
a time frame for completing it. (See verse 6.)

You need to seriously ask yourself the same question: "What
is it that I want?" Do you know what you really want out of life?
Some people think life begins at retirement, and they miss out
on practically their entire lives. Other people just want to indulge
in self-serving activities. Again, many people just want to own a
bigger house, a newer car, and nicer furniture. But, in Luke 12:15,
Jesus said, *"A man's life does not consist in the abundance of his possessions"* (NIV84). There is something more important in life than
the "trophies" we like to accumulate.

In order to find your true vision, you must be in touch with
the values and priorities of the kingdom of God. *Your vision should
be something that lives on after you're gone, something that has greater
lasting power than possessions.* People's lives should be changed by
your vision. Lives were changed because of Nehemiah's vision.
God gave Nehemiah favor: King Artaxerxes granted Nehemiah's
request and provided him with royal protection for his journey.

69

Nehemiah traveled to Jerusalem, and, in spite of opposition, under Nehemiah's supervision, the wall of the city was rebuilt. (See Nehemiah 6.)

"What do you want?" The King of Kings is asking you this question today, and you must be able to give Him an answer. How do you answer His question? First, you ask Him to confirm what He has put in your heart for you to do. In essence, Nehemiah's first response to the problem in Jerusalem was, "Let me go to God in prayer." He had a passion for God and His ways, and he had a burning passion to address the problems of his people. Perhaps you know what this burning is like. You feel frustrated about certain things you see in your neighborhood and your country. You have a strong desire to see change, and you have prayed, "God, something's wrong with our neighborhood, something's wrong with our country." Nehemiah went to God, and God heard his prayer and answered it by confirming what he should do. Your vision uniquely belongs to you as a person called by God. As you seek God, your vision will become clear to you.

ACTION STEPS TO FULFILLING VISION

+ Have you truly answered the King's question "What is it that you want in life?" Write down your answer.

+ What things in your life are distracting you from the real "business"—the true vision—of your life?

⌒

Thought: Your vision should be something that lives on after you're gone, something that has greater lasting power than possessions.

Reading: Nehemiah 2

— DAY 32 —
PRINCIPLE 2: KNOW YOUR POTENTIAL FOR FULFILLING VISION

"Now to him who is able to do immeasurably ["exceeding abundantly" KJV] more than all we ask or imagine, according to his power that is at work within us." —Ephesians 3:20

The second principle for fulfilling personal vision is that *you will never be successful in your vision until you truly understand your potential.* Recall that your potential is determined by the assignment God has given you to do. Whatever you were *born* to do, you are *equipped* to do. Moreover, resources will become available to you as you need them.

What this means is that God gives ability to fulfill responsibility. Therefore, when you discover your dream, you will also discover your ability. God will never call you to an assignment without giving you the provision for accomplishing it. If you understand this principle, no one can stop you from fulfilling your vision.

You must come into an awareness of your potential. Potential is hidden capacity, untapped power, unreleased energy. It is all you could be but haven't yet become. Potential is who you really are, in accordance with your vision, even if you don't yet know your true self. Potential is the person who has been trapped inside you because of false ideas—either your own ideas or others' ideas—about who you are.

God has created you to do something wonderful, and He has given you the ability and resources you need to do it. Ephesians 3:20 says, *"Now to him who is able to do immeasurably ["exceeding abundantly" KJV] more than all we ask or imagine, according to his power that is at work within us."* Many of us have heard this verse so many times that we think we know it. Yet I don't believe we really understand what it is saying: *"According to his power* [or potential] *that is at work"*—where? *"Within us"*! It doesn't say His power is at work in heaven. It says it is at work in us! God put His vision and His Spirit within us, and that is more than enough potential for our needs.

What are the implications of this truth? It means that what you are able to accomplish has nothing to do with who your parents are or were. It has nothing to do with your past or with physical factors such as your race or appearance. Instead, it has to do with *"the power"* working within you. That power is the mighty power of God's Spirit who lives inside you, enabling you to fulfill the vision He has given you. God's power is at work within you for the fulfillment of your dream.

∽

Thought: When you discover your dream, you will also discover your ability to fulfill it.

Reading: Exodus 3

— DAY 33 —

RECOGNIZE YOUR ABILITY

"Then the LORD reached out his hand and touched my mouth and said to me, 'I have put my words in your mouth.'"
—Jeremiah 1:9

Earlier, we read how God told Jeremiah, *"Before I formed you in the womb I knew you, before you were born I set you apart; I appointed you as a prophet to the nations"* (Jeremiah 1:5). Notice that God used the past tense. He had already set apart and appointed Jeremiah as a prophet. Yet, at first, Jeremiah responded, *"I do not know how to speak"* (verse 6). God's reaction was, in effect, "Do not say that! If I built you to be a prophet, don't tell Me you can't talk!" (See verses 6–7.)

Once God showed Jeremiah why he was born, Jeremiah discovered what he could do. In other words, when Jeremiah understood his vision, he began to realize his ability. At first, he didn't think he could speak publicly for God. Whatever God calls for, however, He provides for. Whatever He requires of us, He enables us to do. In this case, God gave Jeremiah the ability to speak for Him: *"Then the LORD reached out his hand and touched my mouth and said to me, 'I have put my words in your mouth'"* (Jeremiah 1:9).

God will give you a dream, and He will also provide for every aspect of its fulfillment. He will never call you to do something that He hasn't already given you the ability to do or that He won't give you the ability to do when the time comes. You shouldn't allow any other human being to judge your potential. Whatever God is causing you to dream is a revelation of your ability.

So, let me ask you again: What do you imagine doing as your life's vision? Go on a "tour" of your dream. As you do, begin to recognize your potential. God gave us the gift of imagination to keep us from focusing only on our present conditions. I don't think we can even begin to imagine all the things God wants to do through us. He wants us to take a tour of our visions on a regular basis. Visit everything. Check out the details of your dream and see its value. Then come back to the present and say, "Let's go there, God!"

Thought: God will never call you to do something that He hasn't already given you the ability to do or that He won't give you the ability to do when the time comes.

Reading: Exodus 4

— Day 34 —

PERFECT FOR YOUR PURPOSE

"For we are God's handiwork, created in Christ Jesus to do good works, which God prepared in advance for us to do."
—Ephesians 2:10

Everything about you is determined by your purpose. God built you, designed you, and gave you the right makeup for what He has prepared for you to do. Your heritage and ethnic mix, the color of your skin, your language, your height, and all your other physical features are made for the fulfillment of your vision. You were built for what you're supposed to do. You are perfect for your purpose.

Your ability isn't dependent on what you perceive as your limitations. How many people have made statements such as these: "I don't have enough education"; "I can't speak well"; "I'm too short/tall"; "I'm part of a minority group"? They have a long list of reasons why they can't do what they are dreaming. None of those excuses is valid. Everything God gave you to do, you are able to do. Everything God put in your heart to do, you have the corresponding ability to accomplish.

Dreams are given to draw out what's already inside us and to activate God's power to enable us to achieve our visions. God may give us dreams that are bigger than our education levels or backgrounds. For instance, I shouldn't be able to do what I am currently doing, based on my background and the expectations of the society I grew up in. Likewise, you may not have the background to do what you are going to do. Other people may not believe you can do it, but, in the end, it's what God thinks that matters. Just keep doing what He tells you to do.

God never gives us dreams to frustrate us. He gives us dreams to deliver us from mediocrity and to reveal our true selves to the world. The more I study the Word of God, the more I realize that God appoints, anoints, and distinguishes people. He doesn't like them to get lost in mediocrity. Therefore, He said, in effect, "Abraham, come out. Moses, come out. David, come out. You are lost among the average."

As you think about your God-given potential, consider the following analogy from nature. In creation, God gave trees the ability to reproduce themselves through their seed. By doing this, He was commanding trees to come out of seeds. First, He put the potential for the trees in the seeds. Then He told humankind, in essence, "If you plant the seeds, putting them in the right environment, those seeds will eventually become what I put in them: their potential, which is fully grown trees."

Our lives are like those seeds. We were born with the potential for the fulfillment of destinies that have already been established within us. Again, when God gives a vision to someone, He's simply calling forth what He put into that person. This is why you can always determine what you can do by the dream that is within you. Plant the seed of your vision by beginning to act on it and then nurture it by faith. Your vision will develop until it is fully grown and bears much fruit in the world.

ACTION STEPS TO FULFILLING VISION

+ If you haven't done so yet, take a "virtual tour" of your dream. Imagine all the details of the completed vision. Then let God know that is where you want to go. Ask Him to enable you to take your idea from dream to full-fledged reality.

+ How can you begin to "plant the seed" of your vision today?

⌒

Thought: Plant the seed of your vision by beginning to act on it and then nurture it by faith.

Reading: Ephesians 2:1–10

PRINCIPLE 3: DEVELOP A CONCRETE PLAN FOR YOUR VISION

"In their hearts humans plan their course, but the LORD *establishes their steps."* —Proverbs 16:9

The third principle for fulfilling personal vision is that *you must have a clear plan.* God gives the vision, but we make the plans. There is no future without planning. I've known people who tried to be successful over and over again without a plan. It never works.

When I was a teenager and had been a Christian for only about two years, I kept wondering why God didn't seem to be guiding me in my life. Perhaps you are wondering the same thing about your own life. I used to want God to show me His will at night in my room, so I would stay up all night with one eye open, just waiting. I used to pray, "Oh, Lord, let the angels show up." Then I would look, and there would be nothing but mosquitoes! Other times, I would hear a little noise outside, and I would open the door thinking that the angels had shown up. Yet, when I looked outside, all I would see was a rat running across the yard. Some angel!

I persisted in wanting God to show Himself to me and to guide me. Whenever we sang a certain song in church, I used to sing it the loudest: "Lead me, guide me, along the way!" One day, as I was singing this song, I felt as if the Lord asked me, "Lead you along *what* way?" I realized then that if you don't have a plan, God doesn't have anything specific to direct you in.

Proverbs 16:1 says, *"To humans belong the plans of the heart, but from the* LORD *comes the proper answer of the tongue."* That's a very powerful statement. God is saying, in effect, "I gave you the vision. Now you put the plan on paper, and I will work out the details."

Proverbs 16:9 says, *"In their hearts humans plan their course, but the* LORD *establishes their steps."* God leaves the planning up to the heart of the person, but He will provide the explanation as to how the vision will be accomplished.

Have you expressed to God what is in your heart, and have you presented Him with your plan for accomplishing it? The Bible says that God will give you the desires of your heart if you will delight in Him. (See Psalm 37:4.) However, it also implies that God will direct the steps to your vision once you make a concrete plan to move toward what you desire.

Thought: God leaves the planning up to the heart of the person, but He will provide the explanation as to how the vision will be accomplished.

Reading: Proverbs 16:1–9

— Day 36 —

IDEAS ARE SEEDS OF DESTINY

"In him we were also chosen, having been predestined according to the plan of him who works out everything in conformity with the purpose of his will." —Ephesians 1:11

Ideas are seeds of destiny planted by God in the minds of humankind according to His will. When ideas are cultivated, they become imagination. Imagination, if it is watered and developed, becomes a plan. Finally, if a plan is followed, it becomes a reality. However, when a person receives an idea from God, that idea must be cultivated soon or it may go away. If that person doesn't ever work on the idea, God will give it to someone else. It's not just having ideas or dreams that is important. Ideas need plans if they are going to manifest in the world.

Young people often think their dreams will just happen. They find out later, after they have sadly wasted years of their lives, that this is not the case. There is no way any of us can move toward our dreams without a plan. Jesus said that a wise person doesn't start to build something unless they first work out the details:

> *Suppose one of you wants to build a tower. Won't you first sit down and estimate the cost to see if you have enough money to complete it? For if you lay the foundation and are not able to finish it, everyone who sees it will ridicule you, saying, "This person began to build and wasn't able to finish."*
> (Luke 14:28–30)

God Himself had a plan when He created humanity. Ephesians 1:11 says, *"In him we were also chosen, having been predestined according to the plan of him who works out everything in conformity with the purpose of his will."*

Someone once said to me, "You always seem to be going somewhere. Just relax." I told him, "I've discovered something about life. Where I live in the Bahamas, when you just sit on a boat in the ocean and relax, the current takes you wherever it's going, even if you don't want to go there. Life is the same way." Too many people float down the current of their lives and still expect to make it to their goals. Instead, we need to be ships with a purpose.

A ship has a compass so that the navigator knows what direction they are going in, and it has a rudder so that the pilot can steer it. Beyond that, a ship is given a specific course—a plan—by the captain, so that it can arrive at its destination. All three are necessary: the compass, the rudder, and the plan. Just because a ship has a rudder doesn't necessarily mean it is going anywhere. It needs to be steered according to the coordinates of the plan.

Likewise, life has given many people clear sailing, yet, because they have no destination, they never make it out of port. What do I mean by "clear sailing"? I mean opportunities. People encounter many opportunities, but they have no plan in place that would enable them to make something out of those opportunities. When the Lord gives you a dream, begin to formulate a plan to fulfill it.

Thought: Ideas are seeds of destiny planted by God in the minds of humankind.

Reading: Proverbs 21:5

— DAY 37 —

YOU WERE NOT DESIGNED TO DRIFT

"But as for me and my household, we will serve the LORD."
                                                    —Joshua 24:15

In Deuteronomy 30:19, God told His people, *"I have set before you life and death, blessings and curses. Now choose life."* In other words, He was saying, "Stop procrastinating and hoping you will eventually get somewhere in life. Decide whether you're going to get a curse or a blessing. Decide whether you're going to die or live." We need to make a decision to follow God's purpose for our lives. Remember what Jesus told the church in Laodicea:

> *I know your deeds, that you are neither cold nor hot. I wish you were either one or the other! So, because you are luke-warm—neither hot nor cold—I am about to spit you out of my mouth.*   (Revelation 3:15–16)

In numerous passages, the Scriptures admonish us that we are responsible for making choices. We must decide between doing good and doing evil. We must decide if we will choose to follow the Creator who designed us or follow after our own ways. Likewise, we must decide if we will embrace our vision and then plan for its accomplishment or take the "easy way" of drifting through life.

In the Old Testament, Joshua made a strong statement about the need to make a decision when he challenged the Israelite people in this way:

> *If serving the LORD seems undesirable to you, then choose for yourselves this day whom you will serve, whether the gods your ancestors served beyond the Euphrates, or the gods of the*

Amorites, in whose land you are living. But as for me and my household, we will serve the Lord. (Joshua 24:15)

Are you going to make a plan, or are you going to procrastinate on your dream and drift along, ending up wherever the lukewarm tide takes you? You were not designed to drift. You were designed for destiny. Make a plan and fulfill it.

⌒

Thought: You were not designed to drift. You were designed for destiny.

Reading: Joshua 24:14–28

— DAY 38 —

THE BLUEPRINT OF YOUR VISION

"In love he predestined us for adoption to sonship through Jesus Christ, in accordance with his pleasure and will."
—Ephesians 1:4–5

When a contractor is building a structure, he uses a blueprint. The blueprint is his plan for his vision, which is the finished building. The contractor always keeps a copy of his blueprint on site with him. Why? He needs to keep checking it to see if the building is being constructed correctly according to the plan. Likewise, if you don't have a plan for your life, you have nothing to refer to when you want to make sure you are on track.

How do you begin developing a blueprint for your vision?

First, you must secure the answer to this very important question: "Who am I?" Until you do, it will be difficult to write a plan for your life because such a plan is directly tied to knowing who you are. You will never become really successful in your life if you don't have a clear idea of your identity in God. For example, the Bible tells us that it is God's pleasure and will for us to be identified as His sons and daughters: *"For he chose us in him before the creation of the world to be holy and blameless in his sight. In love he predestined us for adoption to sonship through Jesus Christ, in accordance with his pleasure and will"* (Ephesians 1:4–5). We are also assured that in God *"we are more than conquerors through him who loved us"* (Romans 8:37).

Many of us have become what other people want us to be. We have not yet discovered our unique, irreplaceable identities. Yet it is knowing your true identity in God that gives you the courage to write your life plan.

Second, to develop a blueprint for your vision, you must answer the question "Where am I going?" Once you learn God's purpose, you can start planning effectively because you will be able to plan with focus. A vision becomes a plan when it is captured, fleshed out, and written down. The plan that's in your heart is a documentation of a future that is not yet finished. When you write down a plan, it's a description of the end of your life, not the beginning. That is why God says, "You make the plan, and I will explain how it can be paid for, who is going to work with it, and where the resources and facilities are going to come from. Leave that part to Me. You just put the plan down."

Have you started developing a plan for your life? Do you know what you want to do next week, next month, next year, five years from now? Can you envision a plan for the next twenty years of your life? God has given you the ability to do that. He has given you a mind, the gift of imagination, the anointing of the Holy Spirit, and the vision of faith. He has also given you the ability to write so that you can record the blueprint you see in your heart. What are you waiting for?

ACTION STEPS TO FULFILLING VISION

+ Do you know the answers to the questions "Who am I?" and "Where am I going?" Start the process of developing a blueprint for your vision by writing your answers to these questions.

+ Start thinking about where you want to be one, five, ten, twenty years from now. Jot down your ideas and continue to think and pray about them.

⌣

Thought: Knowing your true identity in God gives you the courage to write your life plan.

Reading: Romans 8:31–39

— Day 39 —

PRINCIPLE 4:
POSSESS THE PASSION OF VISION

"For the people worked with all their heart."
—Nehemiah 4:6

The fourth principle for fulfilling personal vision is that *you'll never be successful without passion*. Passionate people are those who have discovered something more important than life itself. Jesus told His disciples, in essence, "If you are not willing to take up death and follow Me, then you can't be My disciples; you can't go on with Me." (See Luke 14:27.) He also said, in effect, "If you seek to save your life, you will lose it. Yet if you are willing to lose it for My vision of your life, you will truly live." (See Matthew 16:25.) Giving up false visions and ambitions for your genuine vision is the path to true life.

Are you hungry for your vision? How badly do you want what you're going after? Passion is stamina that says, "I'm going to go after this, no matter what happens. If I have to wait ten years, I'm going to get it." Again, let me say especially to young people that if you want to go all the way to your dream, you can't sit back and expect everything to be easy. You must have purpose that produces passion. You must have the attitude of those who worked on the wall with Nehemiah: *"So we rebuilt the wall till all of it reached half its height, for the people worked with all their heart"* (Nehemiah 4:6).

Remember that after Nehemiah saw in his heart a vision of the rebuilt wall in Jerusalem, he returned to his job, but he was no longer satisfied with it. He was downhearted until he began working on the vision. The dissatisfaction came from his passion for change. I believe that Nehemiah was the kind of man who couldn't hide what he felt. He was sad because he didn't like the way the future looked for his people.

One of the reasons I keep stressing your need for a clear guiding purpose in life is that vision is a prerequisite for passion. The majority of people on the earth really have no passion for life because there is no vision in their hearts. Do you have a vision that produces passion within you?

Thought: Passionate people are those who have discovered something more important than life itself.

Reading: Nehemiah 3

— DAY 40 —

PAUL'S PASSION FOR HIS PURPOSE

"For this purpose I was appointed a herald and an apostle—I am telling the truth, I am not lying—and a true and faithful teacher of the Gentiles."   —1 Timothy 2:7

For this purpose I was appointed a herald and an apostle." Paul knew his purpose in life: God had called him to be an apostle to the Gentiles. In 2 Corinthians, we find a unique passage that shows the burning passion Paul had for his vision. There were some men in the Corinthian church who had challenged Paul's right to call himself an apostle. These challengers were false apostles, yet they attacked Paul's credibility and spiritual qualifications and drew people away from the truth.

Paul responded by addressing the Corinthian believers who were being led away from their faith in Jesus Christ. He wrote that even if what he was about to say sounded ridiculous and foolish at first, he would say it anyway to prove he was an apostle so that they would return to the true gospel:

Are [these other men] Hebrews? So am I. Are they Israelites? So am I. Are they Abraham's descendants? So am I. Are they servants of Christ? (I am out of my mind to talk like this.) I am more.... Five times I received from the Jews the forty lashes minus one. Three times I was beaten with rods, once I was pelted with stones, three times I was shipwrecked, I spent a night and a day in the open sea, I have been constantly on the move. I have been in danger from rivers, in danger from bandits, in danger from my fellow Jews, in danger from Gentiles; in danger in the city, in danger in the country, in

danger at sea; and in danger from false believers.
(2 Corinthians 11:22–26)

Why did Paul give a list of problems and tribulations as part of the proof that he was a genuine apostle? He was saying, in effect, "If the vision and assignment I received weren't real, do you think I'd go through all those hardships?" He paid a price for the vision, but his passion enabled him to do it. Paul reiterated his vision to Timothy: *"For this purpose I was appointed a herald and an apostle—I am telling the truth, I am not lying—and a true and faithful teacher of the Gentiles"* (1 Timothy 2:7).

You are passionate and you are real if you stay steady under pressure. You know your vision is from God when you are still at it once the storm clears. It's easy to get excited about a vision, but it's harder to be faithful to it. Faithfulness to vision is one of the marks of its legitimacy.

∼

Thought: You know your vision is from God when you are still at it once the storm clears.

Reading: Philippians 1:18–25

— Day 41 —

PASSION KEEPS YOU FOCUSED

"So then, King Agrippa, I was not disobedient to the vision from heaven." —Acts 26:19

Paul knew what his purpose in life was, and that is what kept him going through all his struggles. When your vision is from God, nothing can stop you. It doesn't matter if people talk against you. You can even be shipwrecked, beaten, and starved yet still persevere if you are bent on accomplishing your vision. Why did Paul keep getting up every time his opponents whipped, beat, or stoned him? He knew he had to go to the Gentiles in obedience to the vision and command he had received from God. In Acts 26, we have the account of Paul on trial before King Agrippa. Paul summed up his testimony by saying, *"So then, King Agrippa, I was not disobedient to the vision from heaven"* (verse 19).

A crucial aspect of passion is that it helps you to *stay focused on your vision*. You can see this principle at work in churches. Where there is common vision, the people work in harmony. However, wherever there is no vision, there is often fighting, gossiping, murmuring, backbiting, and complaining. When churches are full of complaints, that is evidence that the vision has left them. Vision preoccupies people to the point that they have no time to gossip or get angry at the pastor or complain about his preaching. The same phenomenon can be seen in marriages. One of the reasons why there are so many problems in marriages today is that couples have lost their joint vision. We must rediscover the passion of working together for a common purpose.

If you become passionate about your vision, you can defy the odds, keep your focus, and persevere to the fulfillment of your goals. Whenever you are tempted to quit too soon or to stay down when life knocks you over, remember the examples of Nehemiah and Paul. Capture your vision and stay with it, and you will be rewarded with seeing that vision become a reality, no matter what might try to come against it.

ACTION STEPS TO FULFILLING VISION

+ Ask yourself, "How hungry am I for my vision? How badly do I want what I'm going after?"

+ What evidence of a passion for vision do you see in your life?

+ Do you generally give up the first time you fall down? In what ways might you have become complacent about your vision? What will you do to regain your passion for your dreams?

Thought: If you become passionate about your vision, you can defy the odds, keep your focus, and persevere to the fulfillment of your goals.

Reading: Acts 26:1–23

— Day 42 —

PRINCIPLE 5:
DEVELOP THE FAITH OF VISION

"For we walk ["live" NIV] by faith, not by sight."
—2 Corinthians 5:7 (KJV, NKJV, NASB)

The fifth principle to fulfilling personal vision is that *you must develop the faith of vision.* Earlier, I shared that sight is a function of the eyes, while vision is a function of the heart. I truly believe that one of the greatest gifts God gave humankind is not the gift of sight but the gift of vision.

You have probably heard of the great author and wonderful entrepreneur Helen Keller, who became blind, deaf, and mute as a result of an illness when she was only eighteen months old. She was a powerful, remarkable woman who impacted her whole generation, and she still influences us today. In her old age, she was interviewed by a news anchor about her life. Part of their conversation went something like this: Communicating his questions to her through Braille, the interviewer asked, "Miss Keller, is there anything worse than being blind?" She paused for a moment and, in her unique way of talking, said, "What's worse than being blind is having sight without vision."

What a perceptive woman! Helen Keller, who could not see physically, had more vision and accomplishments than the majority of those in her generation who had sight. Her books are still read today, and her poetry is wonderful. Helen Keller didn't spend her years being angry and blaming God for her blindness and deafness. No, she was able to live a full life because she had vision in her heart. As the saying goes, "Eyes that look are common, but eyes that see are rare."

I am convinced that most people have sight but no vision. As we have learned, physical sight is the ability to see things as they are, while vision is the capacity to see things as they could be—and that takes faith. The Bible says, "As [a person] *thinks in his heart, so is he*" (Proverbs 23:7 NKJV). We must never let what our eyes see determine what our hearts believe. *"For we walk* ["live" NIV] *by faith, not by sight"* (2 Corinthians 5:7 KJV, NKJV, NASB). In other words, we are to walk according to what God has revealed in our hearts.

In the book of Genesis, God told Abraham something that could be seen, believed, and achieved only through the eyes of vision: He told him that inside him was a nation. He and his wife, Sarah, were already elderly, and Sarah had been barren throughout their marriage. However, God said, in effect, "I see a nation in you. Everyone else is looking at your barrenness, but I see a nation of descendants as numerous as the stars in the sky and the sand on the shore." (See Genesis 11:29–30; 12:1–3; 17:1–19.)

Abraham believed God's vision for his life, and that vision came to pass. He became the father of the Hebrew nation and the forefather of the Messiah, Jesus Christ. *"What does Scripture say? 'Abraham believed God, and it was credited to him as righteousness'"* (Romans 4:3).

❧

Thought: Vision is the capacity to see things as they *could* be—and that takes faith.

Reading: Hebrews 11:1–16

— DAY 43 —

FAITH GOD PUTS IN OUR HEARTS

"Faith is the substance of things hoped for, the evidence of things not seen [that you cannot see]."
—Hebrews 11:1 (KJV, NKJV)

When we have vision, we are governed by the faith that God has put in our hearts. Hebrews 11:1 says that *"faith is the substance of things hoped for, the evidence of things not seen* [that you cannot see]" (KJV, NKJV). Therefore, I would define faith as *vision in the heart.* Faith is seeing the future in the present. When you have faith, you can see things you hope to have and achieve.

Remember that sight is the ability to see things as they are, and vision is the ability to see things as they could be. I like to go a step further and define vision in this way: vision is the ability to see things as they *should* be.

Our spirits were designed to operate as God operates. In Genesis 1:26, God said, *"Let us make mankind in our image, in our likeness."* The word *"image"* refers to moral and spiritual character, while the phrase *"in our likeness"* means "functioning like." In other words, we were created to live according to the nature of God and to function as He functions in the world.

Maybe you are going through a hard time right now and you're disheartened. You've lost your vision edge. Perhaps this is because of your surroundings. Sometimes, the environments we live in are not the best for fostering vision. What people say to us is not always encouraging and can be very *discouraging.* We must keep our visions constantly before us because *the visions in our hearts are greater than our environments.* Remember, God gave us vision so we would not have to live by what we see.

The Bible is very clear that *"without faith it is impossible to please God"* (Hebrews 11:6). If you try to function in any way other than by faith, you will malfunction. That is why worry is ungodly and fear makes your vision short-circuit. You were never meant to be afraid.

Jesus was filled with faith, and He was the calmest person on earth. He slept soundly in the middle of a storm. When His frightened disciples woke Him up, He asked them, *"Do you still have no faith?"* (Mark 4:40). He was telling them, "If you have faith, then you, too, will be able to sleep during a storm." You may be saying, "This doesn't sound very practical." It is, however.

I have lived this way—by faith instead of fear—for decades. I don't worry for very long about anything because I believe that, ultimately, everything is on my side. Even the schemes of the devil work to my benefit. All things work together for my good because I am called according to God's purpose. *"And we know that in all things God works for the good of those who love him, who have been called according to his purpose"* (Romans 8:28).

⌒

Thought: Vision is the ability to see things as they *should* be.

Reading: Hebrews 11:17–40

— Day 44 —

THE CREATIVE POWER OF FAITH

"I am watching over My word to perform it."
—Jeremiah 1:12 (NASB)

How does faith work? To answer this question, let's look closely at how God functions. In Jeremiah 1:12, God declared, *"I am watching to see that my word is fulfilled."* The *New American Standard Bible* says it this way: *"I am watching over My word to perform it."* God always brings His words into being.

What did God use to create the universe? He used words. All through the account of creation, we read, *"God said"* (Genesis 1:3, 6, 9, 11, 14, 20, 24, 26). God had an idea for the universe, and then He saw or visualized it. Finally, *He spoke His idea into existence.* The result was that everything God saw in His mind's eye for the earth and the rest of the universe became visible reality in the physical world. God created everything by speaking His thoughts into being.

Thoughts are more important than words because words are produced from thoughts. However, while thoughts are the most *important* things on earth, words are the most *powerful.* This point is crucial to understand because while thoughts design a future, words create that future. Nothing happens until you start talking about it. You can think about something for twenty years, but that will not bring it to pass. Creative power is not in thoughts alone. It is in the words (and actions) that come from them. Whether those words are spoken or written, they are full of creative power to help bring that vision to fruition.

However, you can also undermine your vision if you continually speak negative words about yourself, such as "I'm slow," "I'm not intelligent," "I'm a timid person," or "I'm a failure." You will become everything you constantly declare about yourself. That is the power of words. Compounding this problem is the fact that the devil knows God and His ways very well. Satan knows that the key to creating anything is to have a clear vision of it and to speak it into existence. He wants you to speak negative rather than positive things so that your effectiveness for God's kingdom will be negated. We can help protect our visions by guarding what we say. Proverbs 21:23 tells us, *"Whoever guards his mouth and tongue keeps his soul from troubles"* (NKJV).

If you want to fulfill your vision, you must speak differently than you have been doing. Speak positive things about your life and your vision according to God's Word. Then pray, "Lord, please perform Your Word." You have to speak. A vision doesn't have any power until you talk about it.

⌒

Thought: When you speak or write words expressing what you see in your vision, those words are full of creative power to help bring that vision to fruition.

Reading: Isaiah 55:10–11

— DAY 45 —

FAITH SEES PROBLEMS AS OPPORTUNITIES

"As [a person] *thinks in his heart, so is he."*
—Proverbs 23:7 (NKJV)

Some years ago, a pastor said to me, "Dr. Munroe, I am from Vermont, and there isn't anything up there. There is nothing but maple trees, cows, and snow. There isn't anything happening in the town where I'm from, and I want to do something for God. I'm going to move down south, build a nice church, and do a work for God." I listened to him for a while and then said, "Think about it. You have a great opportunity to build the most dynamic church in Vermont." He looked at me and said, "Yeah!" Today, he has the largest church in his town. We must not only have sight but also vision. When you begin to see with the eyes of faith, you will understand how to make your vision a reality.

You can see every problem as an opportunity for ministry, service, or business. That is really how Bahamas Faith Ministries International got started. The number one problem of people in developing nations is ignorance. God raised up BFMI to be one of the solutions to that problem: to bring knowledge, training, and information to the Third World. The organization was birthed to help solve a problem that affects 3.8 billion people.

A vision is an idea that is so powerful, it should outlive you. In order for that to happen, however, you can't keep your ideas to yourself. You must clearly conceive and express them. I'll never forget the time I was grappling with the possibility of writing books. Publishers had been telling me, "You have many ideas that need to be shared with millions of people. Why don't you write a book?" At first, I responded, "I don't want to write a book. I'm happy just teaching." Then, one night, when I was preparing my notes for a meeting, I felt as if the Lord was saying to me, "If you do not write, what you know will die with you. If you write down the ideas that I have given you, however, your words will live on after you are gone."

Your success or failure is determined by how you see. Jesus continually dealt with the "sight problems" of the disciples because their sight got them into trouble so often. He wanted them to move from sight to vision, and that is why He taught them about faith through life illustrations such as the fig tree, the feeding of the five thousand, and the raising of Lazarus. (See, for example, Matthew 21:19–22; Mark 6:34–44; John 11:1–44.)

The faith of vision is crucial because the way you see things determines how you think and act and, therefore, whether or not your vision will become reality. Proverbs 23:7 declares, "As [a person] *thinks in his heart, so is he*" (NKJV). Do you have sight or vision?

ACTION STEPS TO FULFILLING VISION

- What is your answer to the question "Do you have sight or vision?"
- Are you thinking and speaking in positive or negative terms in relation to your vision?
- Choose one aspect of your vision and practice speaking words of faith regarding it.

Thought: The faith of vision is crucial because the way you see things determines how you think and act.

Reading: 2 Corinthians 4:16–18

PRINCIPLE 6:
UNDERSTAND THE PROCESS OF VISION

*"Let us not become weary in doing good, for at the proper time
we will reap a harvest if we do not give up."* —Galatians 6:9

The sixth principle for fulfilling personal vision is that *you must
understand the process of vision.* God has a plan for each of us, yet
He brings those plans to pass in a gradual way. I'm learning that
God tells us where we are going with our visions, but He rarely
tells us exactly how He will take us there. He gives us purpose but
doesn't explain the full process.

Proverbs 16:9 says, *"In their hearts humans plan their course,
but the LORD establishes their steps."* Notice the word *"steps."* God
didn't say He would direct our leaps but rather our steps. There
is no hurried way to get to God's vision. He leads us step-by-step,
day-by-day, through tribulations, trials, and character-building
opportunities as He moves us toward our dreams. Why does God
lead us in this way? Because He doesn't want us only to win; He
wants us to win with style. God's desire is to fashion people with
character and battle scars who can say, "God didn't just hand me
this vision. I have qualified for it."

Sometimes we become impatient with God's process because
we can see our destinations, and we want to arrive there tomorrow.
However, God says, "No, I have a route that will get you there."
Even though this route may seem long, it is not designed to keep us
from our destinations; *it is designed to prepare us for them.*

At the time when we receive our visions, we are not yet ready
for them. We don't have the ability to handle the big things that
we're dreaming. We don't have the experience or the character

for them. God could accomplish quickly what He desires to do through us, but He wants to prepare us to receive and work in our visions.

You must learn to train for what God has already told you is coming. You don't need to worry about whether or not it is going to come. If He has promised that it is coming, then it is. Remember what we read earlier in the Scriptures: *"For the revelation awaits an appointed time; it speaks of the end and will not prove false. Though it linger, wait for it; it will certainly come and will not delay"* (Habakkuk 2:3). Still, you must stay on course if you're going to follow the work God has called you to do. Stay in the seat where God has placed you, put on your seat belt, and hang on until He brings the vision to pass. It will be realized, but you must wait on Him.

Thought: God tells us where we are going with our visions, but He rarely tells us exactly how He will take us there.

Reading: 2 Peter 1:3–8

— DAY 47 —

BUILDING OUR CHARACTER

"Not only so, but we also glory in our sufferings, because we know that suffering produces perseverance; perseverance, character; and character, hope." —Romans 5:3–4

Sometimes the road to fulfilling our vision takes us through difficulties, both large and small. We ask God, "Why do I need to go this way? I don't like this route." He answers that the route is going to do two things for us:

1. Develop our character

2. Produce responsibleness in us

We weren't born with those things, so we have to learn them. Moreover, if God were to show us the route to where we are going, we might say, "That's okay, God. You can keep the vision. I'll stay right where I am."

The life of Joseph is a great example of this. When he was only seventeen years old, he had a dream from God in which his father, mother, and brothers were kneeling down before him. (See Genesis 37:9–10.) Joseph thought to himself, "Yes! I like this dream." He saw himself up on a throne with a whole kingdom at his feet. In his mind, he was King Joseph.

God had given him a vision, yet He didn't tell him how he was going to get there. Suppose the Lord had said, "Joseph, you're going to become a great ruler, and here is what I have planned to get you there. First, your brothers are going to tear your favorite clothes right off your back. Second, they are going to throw you into a pit. Third, they are going to sell you as a slave. Fourth, your master's wife is going to lie about you, accusing you of rape. Fifth, your master is going to have you put in jail, where you will be forgotten for a long time. However, eventually, you'll get there." If the Lord had said that, Joseph probably would have replied, "I'll just stay a shepherd. I'm very happy where I am right now."

Some of you are in the midst of the vision process and are wondering, "Where is the vision God promised me? Where are all those big dreams He showed me five years ago?" You are beginning to wonder if there is a God in heaven. Joseph likely felt the same way during his ordeals. He found himself sitting in a pit when, just a few days earlier, he had seen himself on a throne. He was probably thinking, "Where is the God who showed me that dream?" I believe God's reply to Joseph was something like this: "I'm with you in the pit, and I'm working on your character because you can't rule well without it."

Suppose Joseph hadn't learned self-control through all his hardships? When Potiphar's wife tried to seduce him, he might have given in to the temptation. Instead, because he had had to learn discipline and reliance on God, he could be trusted in such a situation. God's ways of getting us where we need to go are often different from what we expect, but He always has a reason for them.

⌇

Thought: We weren't born with character or a sense of responsibility, so we have to learn them.

Reading: Colossians 1:9–14

— DAY 48 —

"ISN'T THERE ANY OTHER WAY?"

"It is good to wait quietly for the salvation of the LORD."
—Lamentations 3:26

As you move toward the fulfillment of your vision, you may not face a life-or-death situation, as some of God's people have, but you will have challenges and difficulties to some degree. That is why I want you to be aware of the process of vision and be prepared for it. We often think that because we're going through difficult times, God has stopped working to fulfill our purposes. Yet they are still coming. God is preparing us for our purposes through the process. Often, we sit back and say, "Why do I have to go through all this?" That attitude of complaint and lack of faith is exactly what God is trying to work out of us. He doesn't want us to go into our promised land dragging bad attitudes behind us. He is working for our good.

What if God had said to Moses, while he was still one of the most powerful men in Egypt as the adopted son of Pharaoh's daughter, "I have raised you up to be a deliverer to bring My people out of Egypt into the promised land, but this is how it will transpire: In your zeal to protect My people, you will rashly murder an Egyptian, and you will have to flee into the wilderness and become a mere shepherd. Then, when you become the leader of the Israelites, they are going to infuriate you. They are going to murmur and complain, even revolt against you. As a matter of fact, because of your reaction to them, you will disobey Me, and you won't even make it into the promised land." I think Moses would have said, "Lord, You can keep both the people and Pharaoh. I think I'll pass on this vision."

Or consider the life of Jesus. When the Son of God was very young, wise men came to visit Him. They bowed down before Him, calling Him a king. Yet what a process He had to go through to get to that throne! In the garden of Gethsemane, Jesus began to feel the burden, and He prayed, in effect, "Isn't there any other way?" (See Matthew 26:36–44.) He felt what you are feeling. You might say, "Isn't there any other way to start my business?" God will answer, "No. This is the way I am taking you. This is your route. I want you to start by working in this business. I'm working on your character and your training." Sometimes, we want the vision without being qualified for it.

Lamentations 3:26 tells us, "*It is good to wait quietly for the salvation of the LORD.*" I don't want you to give up on your vision prematurely. God will continually fulfill a little more of your dream until it comes to pass. It will culminate in His timing. This is the will of God for you.

ACTION STEPS TO FULFILLING VISION

+ How has God used experiences in your life to build character in you?

+ What character qualities has God shown you that you need to work on?

+ List ways in which your job is preparing you for your life's work, such as enabling you to develop skills, knowledge, and experience.

⌣

Thought: God is working on us, preparing us for our purposes through the process.

Reading: 1 Thessalonians 5:16–18

—Day 49—

PRINCIPLE 7:
SET THE PRIORITIES OF VISION

"All you need to say is simply 'Yes' or 'No'; anything beyond this comes from the evil one." —Matthew 5:37

The seventh principle of fulfilling personal vision is that *if you want to be successful, you must set priorities for yourself in relation to your vision.* Understanding priority will help you to accomplish your dream because priority is the key to effective decision-making. Both successful and unsuccessful people alike make decisions every day that influence their chances of achieving their visions. Whether they realize it or not, it is the nature and quality of the choices they make that determine their success or failure.

Your life is the sum total of the decisions you make every day. Life is filled with alternatives; we are constantly bombarded with choices, and our preferences reveal who we are and what we value. In fact, you have become what you have decided for the last ten, fifteen, or twenty years of your life. What is perhaps even more significant, you can tell the kind of life you're going to have in the future by the decisions you are making today. In this sense, the future really is now. Sometimes we believe that we can make bad choices today and make up for them later on. That thinking is in error. Whatever we are doing now is our tomorrow.

This is why *yes* and *no* are the most powerful words you will ever say. God wants you to be able to say them with precision because they will determine your destiny. You will be blessed by saying yes to what is in accordance with your vision and no to anything else. In other words, if you want to fulfill your dream, you must fix your eyes on it and not get caught up in anything that won't take you there. You have to know how to maneuver between the alternatives of life, meaning that you have to learn how to prioritize. When people don't succeed in their visions, it is often because they don't understand that prioritizing creates useful limits on their choices.

Since your life is the sum total of the choices and decisions you make every day, you can choose to stay where you are right now, or you can choose to move forward in life by pursuing your dream. I want to challenge you to stop making excuses for why you can't accomplish what you were born to do. Take your life out of neutral. God has given you the power and the responsibility to set priorities to achieve your life's vision.

⁓

Thought: If you want to fulfill your dream, you must fix your eyes on it and not get caught up in anything that won't take you there.

Reading: Matthew 5:33–37

— Day 50 —

WHAT IS BENEFICIAL FOR YOU?

> *"'I have the right to do anything,' you say—but not everything is beneficial."* —1 Corinthians 6:12

In 1 Corinthians 6:12, Paul wrote, *"'I have the right to do anything,' you say—but not everything is beneficial"* (1 Corinthians 6:12). Even though we may have permission to do many things that we want to do, *"not everything is beneficial"* for us. The King James Version uses the word *"expedient,"* which means "appropriate," "suitable," or "desirable." Not everything is advantageous to you. You have to determine what is beneficial, and you define what is beneficial based on the needs of your vision.

The second part of 1 Corinthians 6:12 is a very powerful statement: *"'I have the right to do anything'—**but I will not be mastered by anything.**"* The King James Version reads, *"I will not be brought under the power of any."* The Greek word translated *"power"* means "to control." Even though you can do anything in life, the only things that should master you are the things that line up with God's Word and ways—and that will lead to your personal vision. Something is beneficial if it relates to what you want to accomplish and takes you to your goal. Ask yourself, "What benefits me? What will move me toward my purpose?"

Obviously, the first thing that you would consider as beneficial is your relationship with God. If you want to know where you're supposed to go in life, you have to establish a connection with the Person who gave you the assignment, who created you. It's no wonder the Bible says the greatest commandment is to love God first with all your heart, mind, soul (will), and strength. (See Mark 12:30.) When you do that, He reveals to you the assignment that you were born to fulfill. Once you are certain of where you are meant to go in life and have truly committed to it, then a lot of the extraneous things will fall away on their own.

After you capture your vision, you need to prioritize your life in keeping with that vision. You have to determine how many of the things that you are currently involved in are beneficial to your dream. Those pursuits and activities that are beneficial to your vision become your true priorities.

~

Thought: You have to determine what is beneficial for your life, and you define what is beneficial based on the Word of God and the needs of your vision.

Reading: 1 Corinthians 10:23–31

—Day 51—
KEEP YOUR EYES ON THE MARK

"I press on toward the goal to win the prize for which God has called me heavenward in Christ Jesus." —Philippians 3:14

Sometimes our greatest challenge is not in choosing between good and bad but choosing between *good* and *best*. Thankfully, *the vision itself* helps you decide what is best for you. You do things that are right for your vision. A vision protects you from being misguided by good alternatives. It allows you to say no to lesser opportunities—even if there are certain benefits to them—and to stay focused on what will bring you the best results.

When I was in Israel, our group spent an afternoon visiting a kibbutz. A kibbutz is a self-sufficient community. Everything the people need to live is found right there on the farm. As I walked the grounds and saw the fields where the people grew their own food, I noticed that their tractors and combines were very modern. Then I saw a little field in a valley not far away where a man was working with just an ox hooked up to a plow.

I was intrigued, so I asked one of the men at the kibbutz, "What's he doing?" He answered, "Well, he's planting seeds in his field right now. As the ox makes the furrow, he drops the seeds into the earth." I said, "He's using an animal and an old, outdated plow, but his field is just as perfect as yours, and you use modern machinery!" The man told me, "That guy's system is better than mine! Here's how he keeps his furrows completely straight. First, at the end of the field, he sets up little sticks, and he ties red or white flags on them. Then he goes back to the opposite end of the field, where he starts to plow. He sets his eyes on the little piece of cloth at the far end of the field as he controls the movements of the ox. If he didn't use the sticks, his furrows would be crooked."

What he said next really put the whole thing into perspective for me: "That little stick is called 'the mark.'" This term took me back two thousand years to that same country and that same area, where Jesus had lived, and I understood what Jesus meant in Luke 9:62: *"No one who puts his hand to the plow and looks back is fit for service in the kingdom of God."* When you set your hand to the plow, you must put your eyes on the mark and not look to the left or to the right because you will inevitably move toward whatever you are looking at.

Thought: Sometimes our greatest challenge is not in choosing between good and bad but in choosing between *good* and *best*.

Reading: Philippians 3:7–14

— Day 52 —

DON'T THROW OFF SELF-CONTROL

"Like a city whose walls are broken through is a person who lacks self-control." —Proverbs 25:28

As we have already seen, Proverbs 29:18 is a key verse with regard to vision: *"Where there is no vision, the people perish"* (KJV). This verse is quoted often, though many people do not fully understand it. In Hebrew, the word translated *"perish"* means "to throw off constraints." The *New International Version* reads, *"Where there is no revelation, people cast off restraint."* In effect, this means, "Where there is no vision, the people throw off self-control." If you don't have vision, there are no real restraints in your life. Yet when you have vision, you are able to say no with dignity.

You will never be disciplined in your life until you have real vision. Vision is the key to an effective life because when you see your destination, it helps you to discipline your life in ways that train, prepare, and provide for your vision. Choose to live well. Associate with people and be involved in activities that are conducive to your dream.

How disciplined is your life in relation to your dream? To develop discipline and self-control, ask yourself questions such as the ones below.

ACTION STEPS TO FULFILLING VISION

+ "What am I using my energies on?" What are you putting your heart and soul into? Is it worth it, based on your purpose?

+ "Where am I investing my money?" Your vision dictates where you put your resources. Are you buying things that you don't need or can't afford? Are you so much in debt that you can't channel your money toward fulfilling the vision in your heart?

+ "Which movies, television programs, and books am I spending time on?" Are they hindering or helping you? Do they waste your time or draw you into inappropriate behavior? If you know where you are going, you will choose to engage in things that help you in the knowledge or skills you need for your vision; you will invest that time in your future.

+ "What am I taking into my body?" There are talented, gifted people who are dying prematurely because they consistently eat food that isn't good for them. If you're going to make it to the end of your vision, you must take care of your health.

+ "What am I risking?" Are you abusing alcohol, drugs, or sex? If so, it will certainly short-circuit your vision. Not only is this behavior contrary to God's Word, but it will also sabotage the fulfillment of your life's dream. You must protect your vision.

+ "What is my attitude toward life?" If you know where you're going, you can keep your attitude positive. When things go wrong, you can say, "That's okay. This is only temporary. I know where my true destination is."

⌒

Thought: If you don't have vision, there are no real restraints in your life. Yet when you have vision, you are able to say no with dignity.

Reading: Galatians 5:22–25

PRINCIPLE 8: RECOGNIZE PEOPLE'S INFLUENCE ON VISION

"Come, let us rebuild the wall of Jerusalem, and we will no longer be in disgrace."   —Nehemiah 2:17

The eighth principle for fulfilling vision is that *you must recognize people's influence on your vision.* We need other people if we are going to be successful in life because, as I emphasized earlier, we were not created to fulfill our visions alone. As a matter of fact, God specifically said about His first human creation, *"It is not good for the man to be alone"* (Genesis 2:18). We need people to make it in life. Remember, individual purpose is always fulfilled within a larger or corporate purpose. It is vital that we work with others in making our visions a reality.

When Nehemiah went to Jerusalem to rebuild the city's walls, he said to the people who were living in the decimated city, *"You see the trouble we are in: Jerusalem lies in ruins, and its gates have been burned with fire. Come, let us rebuild the wall of Jerusalem, and we will no longer be in disgrace"* (Nehemiah 2:17). Nehemiah was the one who had received the vision, but he had to go to other people for help in getting it done. For any vision that you have, God has people prepared to work with you, and they will be a blessing to you.

There will always be a need for positive people in your life. When I went to college, I had a dream to get my degree, and there were people who already had been set apart to help me get through it. Some of them helped me academically, others financially, others with encouragement in my spiritual walk. When you have a dream, that's the way it works. People will always be there, waiting to help you. Therefore, if you have no dream, or if you do not begin to act on it, the people who are supposed to help you won't know where to find you.

However, be aware that the principle of influence has a twofold application: people can have a negative effect on us as well as a positive one. When you begin to act on your vision, it will stir up both those who want to help you and those who want to hinder you. Like Nehemiah did, you must respond wisely when you encounter people who would seek to hinder you and your endeavor:

> When word came to Sanballat, Tobiah, Geshem the Arab and the rest of our enemies that I had rebuilt the wall and not a gap was left in it—though up to that time I had not set the doors in the gates—Sanballat and Geshem sent me this message: "Come, let us meet together in one of the villages on the plain of Ono." But they were scheming to harm me; so I sent messengers to them with this reply: "I am carrying on a great project and cannot go down. Why should the work stop while I leave it and go down to you?" Four times they sent me the same message, and each time I gave them the same answer.
>
> (Nehemiah 6:1–4)

Thought: For any vision that you have, God has people prepared to work with you, and they will be a blessing to you.

Reading: Exodus 17:8–13

— Day 54 —

VISION WAKES UP OPPOSITION

"And he did not do many miracles there because of their lack of faith."   —Matthew 13:58

As we saw in the example of Nehemiah, when you act on your vision, it can wake up opposition. It is an interesting phenomenon that certain people will be resistant when you step out and start to do something that they themselves have never done. Some people might resist you because they don't believe you can do it. Other friends and associates might not want you to break out of your current situation because they are afraid you will leave them behind. You need to get used to the idea that people may gossip about you and even treat you with malice because of your vision. It's all part of the process. It is often proof that you're really doing something worthwhile with your life.

Sad to say, sometimes the people who are the most detrimental to the fulfillment of your vision are members of your own family. Some family members may be extremely supportive, but others may not be. This may be because they have lived with you for such a long time that they think they know who you are, so they try to talk you out of all your dreams. When you step outside what others expect you to be, they begin to see you as a problem. Your mother may say, "You'd better stay at your job. It's secure, and it has benefits." Your cousin may say, "What are you leaving your job for? That's good money." These are forms of attack on your vision, even if they are well-intentioned.

Many people want you to be what they want you to be, not what you were born to be, and often they end up limiting you. For example, a family member may say, "I know you—you're just like your mother. She never had any business sense. What do you mean you're going to open a store?" However, people who change the world have declared independence from other people's false expectations. That's what makes them successful. Keep your eyes on the mark, continue working, and keep on building. Your passion has to be more powerful than the opposition of those around you. You must be clear about what you're going to do and persevere in doing it. Be strong and stay encouraged.

⌣‿⌣

Thought: People who change the world have declared independence from other people's false expectations.

Reading: Matthew 13:54–58

— DAY 55 —

THE LAW OF ASSOCIATION

"Walk with the wise and become wise, for a companion of fools suffers harm." —Proverbs 13:20

The law of association states that you become like those with whom you spend time. We often underestimate others' influence in our lives. Often, you don't know you're being influenced until it is too late. Whether you realize it or not, however, the influence of those you spend time with has a powerful effect on how you will end up in life, on whether you will succeed or fail.

You should generally choose friends who are going in the same direction you are and who want to obtain the same things you do, so you can reinforce one another. In light of this truth, I want you to ask yourself three questions.

First, "With whom am I spending time?" Who are your closest friends; who are the people you are confiding in?

Second, "What are these people doing to me?" In other words, what do they have you listening to, reading, thinking, doing? Where do they have you going? What do they have you saying? How do they have you feeling? What do they have you settling for? That last question is an especially significant one because your friends can make you comfortable in your misery. Most important, what is being around these people causing you to become? Solomon said, *"Walk with the wise and become wise, for a companion of fools suffers harm"* (Proverbs 13:20). The *New King James Version* reads, *"The companion of fools will be destroyed."* My version of this maxim is, "If you want to be a success, don't keep company with those who aren't going anywhere in life."

Friends can sometimes put pressure on us, and we end up making wrong decisions. For example, a friend may tell us, "I traded my car in for a brand-new one. You should do the same thing. You have to look right, you know." You give in to the pressure, and the result is that you're knocked right off your goals—your car payments are so high that you can't save money anymore. Don't let anyone throw you off course. Decide for yourself, "What are my goals and plans?" and don't let others influence you to deny them.

Third, ask yourself, "Is what other people are doing to me a good thing in relation to my vision?" When you start telling people where you're going to go and what you're going to do, they may (even unconsciously) begin to say things to try to hinder your dream.

You need to ask yourself and answer these three questions truthfully—and regularly—as you progress toward your vision.

Thought: Whether you realize it or not, the influence of those you spend time with has a powerful effect on how you will end up in life.

Reading: Proverbs 13:10–20

— Day 56 —

WHO WILL YOU WALK WITH?

"Can two walk together, unless they are agreed?"
—Amos 3:3 (NKJV)

If you are going to make it to your dream, you are going to have to disassociate yourself from certain people and places. Jesus said, *"If the blind leads the blind, both will fall into a ditch"* (Matthew 15:14 NKJV). He was telling us not to be foolish by following those who are spiritually blind. You have to disassociate yourself from people who aren't going anywhere and don't want to go anywhere in life. It is crucial for you to guard your heart, thoughts, attitudes, and ideas from being sabotaged by those around you.

So, choose the people in your life carefully. Young people, tell your former companions who were an unhealthy influence on you, "I don't do that any longer. I don't want you coming here. We aren't going in the same direction anymore." There are many people I went to school with that I had to stop spending time with over the years. You can outgrow your friends. When you start pursuing God's vision for your life, sometimes you have to change who your close friends are because you're not speaking the same language any longer. Choose people who want you to go where you want to go. Let them be your encouragement.

You may not want to completely disassociate yourself from some of the people in your life. It is important, however, that you thoughtfully and prayerfully determine how much time you will spend with them. Perhaps there are some people you will just want to be acquainted with, so that you can back off and leave them alone again if you see that being with them causes your vision to falter.

For those of you who are dating and becoming excited about your relationships, please take this to heart: when you have a goal for your life, make sure that the person you are interested in is also interested in your goals. The Bible asks us, *"Can two walk together, unless they are agreed?"* (Amos 3:3 NKJV). Jesus reinforced this theme when He said, *"A house divided against itself will fall"* (Luke 11:17). You don't want to be in a house that is divided. That's what causes confrontation and deep unhappiness. You want to be in a house with one vision.

Thought: Choose people who want you to go where you want to go. Let them be your encouragement.

Reading: Ecclesiastes 4:9–12

— Day 57 —

SPEND TIME WITH PEOPLE OF VISION

"May the God who gives endurance and encouragement give you the same attitude of mind toward each other that Christ Jesus had." —Romans 15:5

For the sake of your life and your vision, you must protect your mental environment. When Paul quoted the adage *"Bad company corrupts good character"* (1 Corinthians 15:33), he was reminding us, "Choose your company well." We all need other people to guide, help, and encourage us along the path to fulfilling our visions. Therefore, as we have been discussing, we must increase the positive influences in our lives and decrease the negative ones while we pursue our individual goals in tandem with others.

If you're going to be successful, you have to spend more time with people who have the same philosophy, standards, and discipline that you do, people who exhibit the kind of character that you want to have. Those are the people with whom you want to expand your relationships.

Who encourages you in the Lord and in your vison? Who can help you toward your goal? What like-minded person can you get close to and learn from? God doesn't want you to spend time listening to critics. He wants you to be encouraged by someone who has already been through the struggles you are going through, because there will be times when you'll feel like giving up. During those hard times, that person can tell you, "You're going to get through it. Don't give up on your dream."

Surround yourself with those who will encourage you in your vision today and every day!

ACTION STEPS TO FULFILLING VISION

+ If you have not already done so prayerfully and honestly, answer the following questions:

    1. "With whom am I spending time? Who are my closest friends; who are the people I am confiding in?"

    2. "What are these people doing to me?" In other words, what do they have you listening to, reading, thinking, doing? Where do they have you going? What do they have you saying? How do they have you feeling? What do they have you settling for?

    3. "Are these people having a positive influence on my life and my vision?"

⁓

Thought: We must increase the positive influences in our lives and decrease the negative ones while we pursue our individual goals in tandem with others.

Reading: Romans 15:1–6

— DAY 58 —
PRINCIPLE 9:
EMPLOY THE PROVISION OF VISION

*"And God is able to bless you abundantly, so that in all things
at all times, having all that you need, you will abound in every
good work."* —2 Corinthians 9:8

T he ninth principle for fulfilling personal vision is that *you must
understand the power of provision.* God is a God of provision. He
is Jehovah-Jireh, "The Lord Will Provide." He provides everything, but He provides it after you begin the work of the vision.
People often stop dreaming about what they really want to do in
life because they know they have few resources with which to do
it. They believe they have to pay for their visions with their present incomes when they can barely make ends meet as it is. When
young people tell their parents what they dream of becoming, the
parents often become nervous because their children's dreams are
too big for them to finance.

If we believe that we have to use our own resources to accomplish God-given visions, then we are small dreamers. I want to
encourage you that the Bible is very clear concerning the dreams
and plans that are in our hearts and how they are meant to be provided for. Remember that Proverbs 16:1 says, *"To humans belong
the plans of the heart, but from the LORD comes the proper answer of
the tongue."* This statement has to do with provision. Whenever a
person receives a dream from God, it usually seems impossible.
Yet God knows that our provisions are never equal to our visions
when we first receive them. He realizes that we cannot explain
to others—or even ourselves—how we are going to accomplish
our visions without the necessary money, people, facilities, or

equipment. He knows that often our dreams are big and our bank accounts are small. What is His solution for us? He says that He will give *"the proper answer of the tongue."*

God's will for our lives comes from His own will. That's why He says *it is our job* to understand, believe, and write down our visions, while *it is His responsibility* to explain how He's going to accomplish them in His time. This frees us to be creative and productive in pursuing our visions. Therefore, if people ask you how you are going to accomplish your dream, you don't have to try to give them a full answer. Tell them you are trusting God for provision each step of the way. Then let God explain to them how it is going to be done. Purpose is your responsibility. Provision is God's responsibility.

~

Thought: God provides everything, but He provides it after you begin the work of the vision.

Reading: 2 Corinthians 9:6–11

—Day 59—

DON'T LET YOUR DREAM CONFOUND YOU

"Praise be to the God and Father of our Lord Jesus Christ, who has [already] blessed us in the heavenly realms with every spiritual blessing in Christ." —Ephesians 1:3

God often gives us dreams so big that they confound us at first because He wants to make sure we don't attempt to fulfill them apart from Him. If we try to do so, we won't succeed, because the strength and resources won't be available. Rest assured that God will never give you a vision without provision. The ability and resources are available for whatever you were born to do. However, as we learned yesterday, our provision is usually hidden until we act on our visions.

I want to show you that everything you need has been provided for you already. Ephesians 1:3 says, *"Praise be to the God and Father of our Lord Jesus Christ, who has [already] blessed us in the heavenly realms with **every** spiritual blessing in Christ."* God has already blessed you with everything you need! Where is it? It is in the heavenly realms, the spiritual world. The next verse starts out with the word *"For."* This tells us that, because of the truth of verse four, verse three is a reality. Before God created you, He already prepared everything you would need so that you could do what you were born to do. He knew what you needed because He chose you for your vision a very long time ago.

One of the reasons we have trouble understanding how God will provide for our visions is that we have a false view of prosperity. We may think prosperity means excess, and that is why we worry when we don't already have money in the bank to fund our visions. Similarly, we may have the idea that prosperity means all our needs should be provided for well ahead of time. Jesus addressed these misconceptions when He told His disciples the following:

> *Therefore I tell you, do not worry about your life, what you will eat or drink; or about your body, what you will wear. Is not life more than food, and the body more than clothes?... So do not worry, saying, "What shall we eat?" or "What shall we drink?" or "What shall we wear?" For the pagans run after all these things, and your heavenly Father knows that you need them. But seek first his kingdom and his righteousness, and all these things will be given to you as well.*
>
> (Matthew 6:25, 31–33)

Do people worry about something they already have? No. Worry isn't related to our present supply. It is related to a perceived or potential lack in the future. Jesus was asking His disciples, in effect, "Why do you want something that you don't need right now? You are focusing on the wrong thing. Seek first God's kingdom and His righteousness, and these things will come with the job. Don't pursue them; they will follow you."

⌒

Thought: Before God created you, He already prepared everything you would need so that you could do what you were born to do.

Reading: Luke 12:22–26

—DAY 60—
THE NATURE OF TRUE PROSPERITY

"Look at the birds of the air; they do not sow or reap or store away in barns, and yet your heavenly Father feeds them."
—Matthew 6:26

To effectively pursue our visions, we must truly understand the nature of prosperity. One of the Hebrew words that is translated as *"prosperity"* in the Bible is *shalev* (see, for example, Psalm 30:6; Psalm 73:3), which means "tranquil," "being at ease," "peaceable," and "quietness." Another Hebrew word for prosperity is *shalom* (see Psalm 35:27; Jeremiah 33:9), which means "peace," "safe," "well," "happy," and "health." The Bible is saying that prosperity is peace. Prosperity is also harmony. When things are in balance, we say they are peaceful. True prosperity means freedom from worry and fear and reflects a state of contentedness that everything necessary is being taken care of.

Jesus used an analogy from nature to help explain prosperity: *"Look at the birds of the air; they do not sow or reap or store away in barns, and yet your heavenly Father feeds them. Are you not much more valuable than they? Can any one of you by worrying add a single hour to your life?"* (Matthew 6:26–27).

Let's look at the implication of this passage. How does God feed birds? He provides for them, but He doesn't personally hand-deliver food to their nests! When Jesus said that the heavenly Father feeds the birds, He meant that everything they need has been made available for them, but they have to go and get it.

God does not build a bird's nest. He provides the twigs. The bird has to find them, pick them up, and bring them back to the tree it has chosen for a home. God does not leave worms on the top of the ground every morning. The bird has to go digging for them. It has to keep working, working, working until it finishes building its nest. It has to keep working, working, working until it gets the worm. Similarly, you can trust God to provide for you as you work toward your vision.

Another fundamental aspect of provision is that God has designed every purpose with its own prosperity. Here is the key: *true prosperity is directly related to your purpose in life.* The nature and degree of your prosperity are determined by what your assignment is. You were not born to have too much or too little. You were born to fulfill God's purpose. When you capture your vision—the part you're supposed to contribute to your generation and succeeding generations, the role you're supposed to play in history—when you capture that and are pursuing it, you will see that all your provisions are automatically built into it.

In this way, you don't ultimately work for money or food, because you're too busy living. You were not created by God just to pay a mortgage. You were not given life simply to keep food in the refrigerator. In your heart, you know that's true. You were created for a purpose, and God has designed every purpose with its own prosperity. Your purpose has built-in provision for it. God never requires from you what He does not already have in reserve for you.

Thought: True prosperity means freedom from worry and fear and reflects a state of contentedness that everything necessary is being taken care of.

Reading: Matthew 6:25–34

—Day 61—

FOUR WAYS GOD PROVIDES FOR VISION

"It is God who works in you to will and to act according to his good purpose." —Philippians 2:13

In the Scriptures, I have discovered several ways in which God provides the resources—financial and otherwise—that we need to fulfill the visions He gives us.

One way God provides for our visions is through our *ability to obtain and use land* and the resources inherent in it. Although real estate prices fluctuate, there is a special prosperity in owning land. According to the biblical record, land seems to be God's first order of prosperity; it is His concept of wealth. (See, for example, Genesis 2:7–12; 12:1, 6–7; 26:2–4; 28:10–15.) God has also given us the *ability to cultivate land* to increase how we use it for our vision. (See Genesis 2:15.) We can plant on it, build a ministry or business on it, raise a family on it—cultivate it fully for God's purposes.

Another way God provides for our visions is through *our work*. When you decide to move forward with your dream, it often takes a great amount of work. I define work as "the passion that is generated by a purpose." God Himself worked when He created the world, and He still works to carry out His purposes. Philippians 2:13 says, *"It is God who works in you to will and to act in order to fulfill his good purpose."*

Because you are made in God's image and likeness, you are designed to work. Remember that work is meant to include creativity and cultivation, not drudgery. Work was given to humankind before the fall; it was a natural part of their being. Through work, they fulfilled part of their purpose as human beings created in God's image.

A third way God provides for our visions is by giving us *wisdom to preserve and reserve for the future*. For example, Joseph was sent to Egypt ahead of his brothers and his father, Jacob, because God knew a famine was coming, and they would need to be preserved. Don't worry about provision but plan for it. In fact, planning destroys worry. It's when you *don't* plan that you start worrying. We live on the daily bread God gives us, but He also wants us to plan for things. God will bless you, and He will provide for the vision, if you know how to put things on reserve for the future.

A fourth way God provides for vision is by *enabling us to help future generations with their dreams*. God doesn't want only you to enjoy the wealth; He wants your children and grandchildren to enjoy it, too. "*A good person leaves an inheritance for their children's children*" (Proverbs 13:22). What is your vision of inheritance for your descendants?

ACTION STEPS TO FULFILLING VISION

+ Has your definition of prosperity changed as a result of reading the devotions from the last few days? Why or why not?

+ What resources do you need to fulfill your vision? List them, and then trust God to provide for all the needs of your vision as He has promised to do.

⌒

Thought: Through our work, we fulfill part of our original purpose as human beings created in God's image.

Reading: Philippians 4:14–20

— Day 62 —

PRINCIPLE 10: USE PERSISTENCE IN ACHIEVING THE VISION

"Therefore, my beloved brethren, be steadfast, immovable, always abounding in the work of the Lord, knowing that your labor is not in vain in the Lord."

—1 Corinthians 15:58 (NKJV)

The tenth principle for fulfilling personal vision is that *you must be persistent if you are going to achieve the vision God has given you.* As I wrote earlier, you need to realize that obstacles are going to come against you and your vision. Even though God gave the vision, that doesn't mean it's going to be easy to obtain. Please don't think that you are exempt from this reality. Trouble isn't going to say about you, "I guess I'll just leave that person alone." When you decide to be somebody, everything is going to try to get in the way of your vision. You must be prepared for challenges, for they are coming.

Think about it: there's no resistance if you're not moving. People who aren't doing anything have nothing to worry about. If you don't want problems, just don't do anything important in life. However, if you are following your vision and you encounter problems, you can say, "Thank You, Lord; at least I'm moving forward!"

One word that describes God's nature is *faithful.* This is because He is true to what He has decided to accomplish, and nothing can stop Him. (See, for example, Hebrews 10:23.) We need to manifest this characteristic in our own lives as we persist in our visions.

Another word that helps us understand God's nature in relation to His persistence in purpose is *steadfast.* To be steadfast means to stand fast or stand steady in the face of resistance. If you are steadfast, then, when opposition comes, you don't turn and go back where you were. You push forward. Opposition should strengthen your resolve and revive your stamina.

In addition to developing the qualities of faithfulness and steadfastness, we must learn to be *courageous* as we persist in completing our visions. When we have courage, we have the ability to stand up in the face of fear. In fact, it is impossible to have courage *without* fear. Faith always demands that we do something we know we can't do on our own, and this challenge often causes us to be afraid at first. God told Joshua, *"Be strong and courageous"* (Joshua 1:6, 9). Why did He say that? Clearly, Joshua must have been scared! Fear, however, can have a positive effect if it gives birth to courage.

If you're afraid to step out in your vision because it's so big, then let your courage come to life as you trust God. *"Wait for the* LORD; *be strong and let your heart take courage; yes, wait for the* LORD" (Psalm 27:14 NASB). Courage says, "I'm afraid, but I'm still moving." Jesus loves for us to do the impossible because the impossible is always possible with God. (See Matthew 19:26.)

~⁓

Thought: Three qualities that we need to develop as we persist in completing our visions are *faithfulness, steadfastness,* and *courage.*

Reading: Joshua 1

— Day 63 —

VISION CAN OVERCOME CHALLENGES

"Let us run with perseverance the race marked out for us, fixing our eyes on Jesus, the pioneer and perfecter of faith."
—Hebrews 12:1–2

There are many types of challenges and pressures in life. During His time on earth, Jesus showed us how to bring a vision to pass in the midst of such challenges. He faced similar problems and obstacles to those you and I face today, yet His vision came to pass. He is our greatest Teacher for learning how to overcome challenges.

For some of us, life is tough even at the start. Perhaps your parents were divorced when you were just a child. Maybe your father is an alcoholic or your mother is a drug addict. Perhaps you aren't even sure who your father is. Or if you know who he is, you wish you didn't. Jesus knows what it feels like to have a difficult family background because He was called "illegitimate." He was born under what the world considered "questionable circumstances." (See Matthew 1:18–25.) Yet that did not stop Him from knowing His relationship to His heavenly Father and fulfilling His purpose as God's Son. No matter what your background is, your relationship with your Father in heaven will help you overcome your difficult circumstances and fulfill your purpose as His child.

Throughout His life on earth, Jesus went through everything you can imagine. There were people who were against Him, who continually schemed to make Him fail. There were those who liked to set Him up for a fall by asking Him trick questions. A crowd once tried to push Him off a cliff. The religious leaders plotted to kill Him. Do you think people call you names? They called Jesus names too. They called Him demon-possessed. They said He was a glutton and a drunkard. They hit Him with everything. The harshest taunt and the highest evil, however, was when they said He was full of the devil.

How did Jesus overcome? How did He succeed in His vision? How did He finish the work the Father had sent Him to do when He faced all that opposition? Jesus was able to remain composed through all those trials because the vision in His heart was bigger than all the threats, accusations, and insults. He knew how to persevere with a dream. Likewise, the vision in your heart needs to be larger than any opposition that comes against you so that you can persist in your life's purpose. Remember that Jesus understands exactly what you are going through, and He is ready to give you direction and strength.

⌒

Thought: No matter what your background is, your relationship with your heavenly Father will help you overcome your difficult circumstances and fulfill your purpose as His child.

Reading: Hebrews 4:14–16

—Day 64—

STAY IN THE FIGHT

"Fight the good fight of the faith."   —1 Timothy 6:12

Once, when I was staying at a hotel in Israel, I couldn't sleep because I had recently arrived and wasn't yet used to the time difference. At about two in the morning, I was up watching a boxing match on television. It was a twelve-round title match, and the boxer from Mexico was pummeling the boxer from the United States. Every time the American boxer moved forward to fight, the other boxer pounded him.

By the sixth round, the US boxer was getting beaten badly, and at the end of the round, he stumbled back into his corner, sat down on the stool, and sagged as if he were a sack of potatoes. Then I saw something happen. In seconds, several men went to work on him. One grabbed a bucket of water and doused him with it. The next grabbed a soaking-wet sponge and squeezed water all over his face. Another applied ointment to soothe his wounds. These men were all talking to him at once, and they were rubbing him down as they talked. Even though he was getting trounced, they were telling him, "You can do this. You can get back out there. You're strong! You're better than he is!" One of the men said, "Keep your left hook, okay? Keep your left hook. He's a slow left. You can get him with that left." After about two minutes, the boxer jumped up, saying, "Yeah! Oh, yeah!" He ran back out there, and everything changed in the seventh round.

Guess who won the fight? The one who had been about to quit in the sixth round won the fight and received the prize. There was blood everywhere, but under that blood was the champion. When he won the decision, all his strength came back. He ran around the room screaming. When you win, you forget all the pounding you received during the fight.

Sometimes, you will get beaten up pretty badly in life, but *stay in the fight*. Fight until you feel the joy of victory. When you think you're going to lose, and you stumble back into the corner of life, the Lord will come and pour the cool water of His Word on your head. He will take the ointment of the Holy Spirit and bring healing to your wounds. He will rub life back into your spirit so you can jump back out and say, "Hey! Come on, Life!" Just like the boxer's coaching team, the Holy Spirit speaks good things into your spirit, such as *"Greater is he that is in you, than he that is in the world"* (1 John 4:4 KJV). Life will be tough, but get back out there and start throwing blows. Keep your left up. That's persistence.

We know that God wants us to be fighters because the Bible calls us soldiers. (See 2 Timothy 2:3–4.) We are warriors. We are people of battle. The Bible also refers to us as those who *"wrestle"* (Ephesians 6:12 KJV, NKJV). This is because we don't just receive medals from God. We earn them. If God didn't want you to fight, He would have given you the medal without the conflict!

⌒

Thought: Stay in the fight until you feel the joy of victory.

Reading: Ephesians 6:10–17

— DAY 65 —
CHARACTER IS FORMED BY PRESSURE

"You need to persevere so that when you have done the will of God, you will receive what he has promised."
—Hebrews 10:36

Persevere actually means "to bear up under pressure." I like this quote from Eleanor Roosevelt, which actually applies to all people: "A woman is like a tea bag. You never know how strong it is until it's in hot water." Here's a similar analogy: People who are successful are like tea bags. When they get in hot water, they make tea. When life squeezes them, they don't become angry; they do something constructive with the pressure. They persevere under it and use it for their own benefit. People who have vision are stronger than the pressure life brings.

I have discovered that sometimes you don't get the scent from the rose until you crush it. In order to draw the fragrance of His glory from your life, God will allow you to be put under stress. We forget too easily that *character is formed by pressure*. The purpose of pressure is to get rid of what is not of God and to leave what is pure gold.

Perhaps you're in the fire right now. It's a good place to be. Go ahead and make tea. Surprise your enemies with the scent of God. Let them pressure you to release His glory. No matter what people may say about you, don't retaliate. Let them talk about you on your job. It doesn't matter what they think. You can smile, knowing that you will come through the situation. The Scriptures say it is not those who are swift, but those who endure to the end, who succeed. (See Matthew 24:13; Mark 13:13; James 5:11.) *There is no stopping a person who understands that pressure is good for him because pressure is one of the keys to perseverance.*

You must also understand that your vision comes with a cost. I thank God that, earlier in my life, I had the privilege of observing firsthand the cost to another visionary, who told me, "Myles, my son, get ready for the price." Because of that experience, I have been prepared to accept the cost.

At times, you will find it difficult to remain in your vision. I understand. It's tough for me to stay in mine. The demands that God has made on my ministry are high because the call requires it. There's a price. Vision always demands a cost. Someone has to pay the price. Are you willing to do it?

ACTION STEPS TO FULFILLING VISION

+ In what areas of your life/vision are you in need of perseverance?
+ What have you given up on that you need to pick up again and continue on with?
+ Ask God to develop faithfulness, steadfastness, and courage in you.

Thought: The purpose of pressure is to get rid of what is not of God and to leave what is pure gold.

Reading: 2 Thessalonians 3:5

PRINCIPLE 11: BE PATIENT IN THE FULFILMENT OF VISION

"You need to persevere ["have need of patience" KJV]."
—Hebrews 10:36

Principle eleven is that *you must be patient in seeing the fulfillment of your vision.* Even if it takes a while for your vision to come to fruition, if you are willing to wait for it (which many people are not), it will come to pass. The writer of Hebrews tells us, *"Do not throw away your confidence; it will be richly rewarded. You need to persevere ["have need of patience" KJV] so that when you have done the will of God, you will receive what he has promised"* (Hebrews 10:35–36). People who have long patience will always win.

When some people make plans to carry out their visions, they try to force those plans into their own timetable or their own way of bringing them to pass. However, you cannot rush a vision. It is given by God, and He will carry it out in His own time. You may ask, "Then what is the reason for developing a plan in the first place?" Remember that the reason you make a plan is so you can have a plan to modify, as necessary and appropriate, along the way—while still keeping to the overall vision. *Patience ensures the eventual success of your plan.*

We are not all-knowing, as God is. We need to patiently rely on His guidance every step of the way. Remember that He promises to take us step-by-step, not leap-by-leap. Part of that step-by-step process is to make some adjustments to the plan as the working out of His purposes becomes clearer to us. We will learn to follow the subtle leading of the Holy Spirit in our lives in which we *"hear a voice behind* [us], *saying, 'This is the way; walk in it'"* (Isaiah 30:21).

You should always put deadlines on your goals, but you must also be willing to rearrange those deadlines. Be assured that the fulfillment of your vision will come at the right time. God sent Jesus to be our Savior about four thousand years after the fall of humankind. Humanly speaking, that was a long time to wait. But He came just as predicted and at just the right time. The Bible says, *"But when the time had fully come, God sent his Son, born of a woman, born under law, to redeem those under law, that we might receive adoption to sonship"* (Galatians 4:4–5).

Jesus came in the fullness of time, and so will your vision. That is why you need to be patient with your dream as you wait for it with anticipation. If someone asks you about it, say, "I'm just waiting for the next move." Some people might wonder if it will ever happen. You do not need to wonder, however, but simply wait. It will all come to pass if you are willing to progress at the vision's pace.

⌒

Thought: We are not all-knowing, as God is. We need to patiently rely on His guidance every step of the way.

Reading: 2 Peter 3:8–9

— Day 67 —

PATIENCE OVERCOMES ADVERSITY

"But let patience have its perfect work, that you may be perfect and complete, lacking nothing." —James 1:4 (NKJV)

Patience is the key to power over adversity and turmoil. If you threaten someone, and they just wait, your threat is going to wear off. The Bible says that a patient person is stronger than a mighty warrior: *"Better a patient person than a warrior, one with self-control than one who takes a city"* (Proverbs 16:32).

When I first read that verse, I found it hard to believe that patience is more powerful than might. Then I came to understand the power of patience. A patient person makes others unsettled because they want that person to react to them, to become angry— but they never do. Nothing can make you more nervous than a waiting person. You try everything, and all they do is just wait. Their waiting eventually unnerves and overcomes the opposition.

Therefore, when you have true vision, no one can offend you. Do your coworkers dislike you? That's all right. It's just temporary. Are they not speaking to you? That's okay. It's just temporary. Are they trying to hold you back? No problem. It's just temporary. Your job is not your life. It's merely a classroom to prepare you for your future.

Patience wins the race. As long as you can dream, there's hope. As long as there's hope, there's life.

It's crucial that we maintain our dreams by patiently waiting for their fulfillment in the fullness of time. James 1:4 says, *"But let patience have its perfect work, that you may be perfect and complete, lacking nothing"* (NKJV). Others who have gone before us have had their faith tested, and it has produced patience in them (see

James 1:3) so that they were able to win the race. Let us do the same. Hebrews 12:1 says, *"Wherefore seeing we also are compassed about with so great a cloud of witnesses, let us lay aside every weight, and the sin which doth so easily beset us, and let us run with patience the race that is set before us"* (KJV). Amen.

ACTION STEPS TO FULFILLING VISION

- Have you been trying to force the timetable of the fulfillment of your vision? If so, what have you learned about patience in the last two days of devotions that will enable you to trust God to fulfill the vision in His timing?

- Encourage your spirit as you patiently wait for your vision to come to pass by committing these verses to memory this week:

But let patience have its perfect work, that you may be perfect and complete, lacking nothing. (James 1:4 NKJV)

We do not want you to become lazy, but to imitate those who through faith and patience inherit what has been promised. (Hebrews 6:12)

You need to persevere so that when you have done the will of God, you will receive what he has promised. (Hebrews 10:36)

Thought: It's crucial that we maintain our dreams by patiently waiting for their fulfillment in the fullness of time.

Reading: Psalm 40:1–3

PRINCIPLE 12: STAY CONNECTED TO THE SOURCE OF VISION

"I am the vine; you are the branches.... Apart from me you can do nothing."   —John 15:5

Principle twelve is that *if you are going to be successful in your vision, you must have a daily, dynamic personal prayer life with God.* Why is this important? Because it is vital that you have continual communion and fellowship with the Source of vision. Remember that you were born to consult God to find out His purpose for your life so that you can discover your vision. Yet, as *"the Alpha and the Omega, the Beginning and the End"* (Revelation 1:8 NKJV), God is not only the Author of your vision, but also your continuing Support as you progress toward its fulfillment.

You will never achieve your vision without prayer because prayer is what keeps you connected to the Vision-Giver. In John 15:5, Jesus said, *"I am the vine; you are the branches.... Apart from me you can do nothing."* If you stay in touch with God, you will always be nourished in both life and vision.

Sometimes, in the pursuit of your vision, you will grow emotionally and spiritually weary if things don't seem to be working out for you. When you have been pressed, criticized, and opposed, you can become weak in faith. That is when you must stagger back to your prayer closet and say, "God, I want to give up," so that you can hear Him say to you, "What you began will be finished." Philippians 1:6 says, *"He who began a good work in you will carry it on to completion."* Prayer is the place where you can take all your burdens to God and say, "God, I *have* to make it," and He will say, "I'm with you. What are you afraid of?" God will bring you through your difficulties and give you the victory through prayer based on His Word. *"The Lord is my light and my salvation—whom shall I fear? The Lord is the stronghold of my life—of whom shall I be afraid?"* (Psalm 27:1).

Sometimes you will wonder if you are ever going to make it. That's a good time to run to God. In prayer, you get away from the noise and confusion of life and say, "Lord, I'm not going back out there." Yet, if you will let Him encourage and refresh you, by the time you have finished praying, you will be saying, "I'm ready to go again!"

Thought: If you stay in touch with God, you will always be nourished in both life and vision.

Reading: Colossians 4:2

PURPOSE IS THE "RAW MATERIAL" OF PRAYER

"Your kingdom come, your will be done, on earth as it is in heaven." —Matthew 6:10

I am convinced that prayer is one of the most misunderstood arts of the human experience. Prayer is not just an activity, a ritual, or an obligation. Nor is it begging God to do what we want Him to do. It is communion and communication with God that touches His heart. In the garden of Eden, when Adam and Eve sinned and broke their relationship with God, their effectiveness in prayer was also broken. True prayer is maintained through oneness of heart and purpose with God. Only then can we fulfill His ways and plans.

When we pray, we represent God's interests on earth, and representation requires relationship. The difficulties many people have with knowing how and what to pray may be traced to the fall and the resulting fallen nature of mankind, through which we were estranged from God. Even as redeemed believers, we must realize and act upon who we are in Christ and the principles of prayer that God has established if we are to be restored to His purposes in the crucial area of prayer.

We may not think of prayer as being an area in which we need to be *transformed by the renewing of [our] mind* (Romans 12:2). However, since effective prayer has everything to do with being united with God in a relationship of love, having a heart and mind in union with God's will, gaining a discerning mind in regard to His purposes, and exercising faith in His Word, it is a vital area in which we need to be transformed. Prayer should not be open-ended. It should be purpose-driven, motivated by a knowledge of God's ways and intentions.

Praying does not involve convincing God to do your will but doing His will through your will. Therefore, the key to effective prayer is understanding God's purpose and vision for your life, His reason for your existence—as a human being in general and as an individual specifically. This is an especially important truth to remember: *Once you understand your purpose and vision, they become the "raw material," the foundational matter, for your prayer life.* If we ask for things that are contrary to our purpose, we will be frustrated. Jesus always prayed for God's will to be done and then worked to accomplish it.

God's will is the authority of your prayers. Prayer is calling forth what God has already purposed and predestined—continuing His work of creation and the establishment of His plans for the earth.

In this way, your purpose in God is the foundational material for your prayers regarding...

provision	faith
healing	praise
deliverance	thanksgiving
power	confidence
protection	assurance
endurance	boldness
patience	peace
authority	

...for the supply of all your needs.

Everything you need is available to fulfill your vision. All that God is, and all that He has, may be received through prayer.

⌒

Thought: Once you understand your purpose and vision, they become the "raw material," the foundational matter, for your prayer life.

Reading: Matthew 6:5–15

—— Day 70 ——
PRAYER ENCOURAGES YOU IN THE FIGHT

"Rejoicing in hope, patient in tribulation, continuing steadfastly in prayer." —Romans 12:12 (NKJV)

Without prayer, you cannot get where you want to go. There will be times when all you'll have is prayer. You won't have any money, people, or resources—just prayer. Yet that is all you need. The Lord will see you through.

Through our prayers, God encourages us to get back out into the fight of faith. Isaiah 40:31 says, *"Those who hope in the LORD will renew their strength. They will soar on wings like eagles; they will run and not grow weary, they will walk and not be faint."* Yes, you will become tired, and sometimes you will want to quit. However, if you are willing to bear up in prayer and stand before God and say, "God, I'm hoping in You!" He will give you strength.

If people attack your dream, go to God. Again, don't try to explain and give an answer for everything because you can't explain anything to critics. Instead, stay connected to your Source for the renewal of your purpose, faith, and strength, and you will be able to persevere to victory. God is the One who planted your life's purpose within you in the beginning. He has invested Himself in your dream, and He will bring it to pass.

Then, when you achieve your vision, there will be people who will see you enjoying the victory, and they will be proud of what you have accomplished. You'll have your belt on as the "boxing champion." Of course, they won't know about the rounds you lost, how you sometimes staggered as you made your way back into your corner to recuperate for the next round. A real fighter doesn't wear his medals on his chest. He wears them on his back. They are his scars. Only a few people will know what it took for you to achieve your vision. Yet you must be willing to take the scars if you want to wear the crown.

Believe me, every champion does not win every round, but if they persevere, they win the match. Remember, since prayer is where you receive the ability to continue the fight, it is crucial for you to find times during the day when you can go to God and say things like, "God, I'm scared," so that He can reassure you that He is with you. He says, *"Surely I am with you always"* (Matthew 28:20). When you hear that, it is enough.

You can win, you can be victorious, if you are willing to take the obstacles in your life and vision to God in prayer.

ACTION STEPS TO FULFILLING VISION

+ Establish a daily prayer time with God.

+ In what ways are you relying on God for your life and vision? In what ways aren't you relying on Him?

+ Commit to prayer the areas in which you aren't currently relying on Him. Be honest with Him about how you are feeling, and allow Him to strengthen, sustain, and encourage you through His presence and His Word.

⌒

Thought: Stay connected to your Source for the renewal of your purpose, faith, and strength, and you will be able to persevere to victory.

Reading: Ephesians 6:18–20

— DAY 71 —
CHANGE IS NATURAL

"Therefore, if anyone is in Christ, the new creation has come: The old has gone, the new is here!" —2 Corinthians 5:17

Nothing on earth is as permanent as change. Understanding this paradoxical truth transformed my life. It protected me when I was a youth, and it has helped guide me as an adult to keep on track with my vision even when change was all around me.

Change is a principle of life. It is the way the world functions. It is natural to human existence and common to all creation. Everything is in a constant state of change, and nothing can stop it. Change is both evidence that we are alive and proof that we are finite—because everything has its own season, and nothing on this earth lasts forever. The apostle Paul reassured us about the necessity of spiritual and personal change in our lives when he wrote, *"And we all, who with unveiled faces contemplate the Lord's glory, are being transformed into his image with ever-increasing glory, which comes from the Lord, who is the Spirit"* (2 Corinthians 3:18).

Thus, we must recognize that change is inevitable. No one on earth can avoid change. No matter who you are—regardless of your country, race, ethnicity, language, financial standing, or disposition—*time* and *change* will affect you! This conclusion is not easy for some people to accept. Yet when I settled this fact in my own heart and mind, my life became much easier to live. It is not healthy for us to believe that life will always remain the same. Everything may be going on an even plane right now, but there will be a transition or a point of stress in the future. Life is continually handing us personal, family, community, and national changes.

Life is full of the unexpected, and changes will come upon us at one time or another.

In fact, everything that you go through is a manifestation of some type of change, and it's just a part of life. The question we must ask is, how does change affect our visions? To be successful in the changing seasons of life, we need to understand the dynamics of change and determine to respond rather than to react to it. Today's leaders will have to be creative on demand, understanding their roles and purposes in their generation. Be bold and embrace the next season of your life. It's the only path to fulfilling your potential—and making your unique contribution to your generation.

Thought: Change is a principle of life. It is the way the world functions.

Reading: 1 John 3:2–3

— DAY 72 —

CHANGE CAN MAKE THINGS HAPPEN

"Do not conform to the pattern of this world, but be transformed by the renewing of your mind. Then you will be able to test and approve what God's will is—his good, pleasing and perfect will." —Romans 12:2

I have discovered five ways that people typically approach change. In an earlier devotion, we briefly looked at two of these perspectives on life when we discussed how vision gives us passion. The fifth approach below is a powerful aid to your vision, while the first four approaches hinder it.

1. *People watch things happen.* This is a passive, indifferent approach in which people don't react to change because they have no real interest in it or its impact. They are drifters.

2. *People let things happen.* This is a resigned, defeated, or even fatalistic approach. People may lash out against the change, but, ultimately, their mindset is, "There's nothing I can do about this."

3. *People ask, "What happened?"* This is an inquisitive response, but it doesn't go much further than mere curiosity. It can also mean that people never saw the change coming, and therefore they weren't prepared to respond to it.

4. *People defy what happens.* This is when people try to resist inevitable change in their lives, wasting valuable time and energy in the process.

5. *People make things happen.* This is a proactive response that either alters the quality or degree of the change that happens or that initiates new change.

Note that the first four ways are all *reactions* to change. When change happens to you, around you, or within you, you have to be wise in how you deal with it. Many people experience immediate confusion, fear, desperation, or anger when they confront change—and, as a result, they act in negative ways that reflect those feelings. If we are to benefit from change, we must understand our role in the process and work with it rather than against it.

You will never really know who you are—and who you can be—if you don't understand the nature of change and how to shape its consequences. Answer the following questions about your approach to change as you begin to consider whether you are allowing it to work for you or against you:

+ What is your general experience with change in your life?

+ Do you feel that change is working for you—or do you feel that its influences are working against you?

+ Do you know how to turn negative change to your benefit? If you answered yes, in what ways have you done this?

+ To what extent have you been initiating positive change in your life?

⌒

Thought: You will never really know who you are—and who you can be—if you don't understand the nature of change and how to shape its consequences.

Reading: Daniel 2:20–22

ONLY GOD AND HIS PROMISES ARE PERMANENT

"I the LORD do not change."   —Malachi 3:6

The greatest security against the disorientation and disruption of change is our reliance on the unchanging God. The Lord spoke to the prophet Malachi, *"I the LORD do not change"* (Malachi 3:6). God is predictable only in the sense that His nature is unchanging. He is always true to Himself, and He is always true to His Word. We can't count on 100 percent truthfulness from any human being, but we can count on God's truthfulness and faithfulness. Moses declared, *"God is not a human, that he should lie"* (Numbers 23:19).

God is not only unchangeable, but He is also eternal. The Scriptures record that the patriarch Abraham *"called upon the name of the LORD, the Eternal God"* (Genesis 21:33). Eternity is not ruled by time. God exists outside of time, although He interacts with human beings and human affairs within the realm of time.

Our world functions in time because God created it to function in that way. The purpose of time is clearly stated in the biblical account of His creation of the world: *"And God said, 'Let there be lights in the expanse of the sky to separate the day from the night, and let them serve as signs to mark seasons and days and years'"* (Genesis 1:14 NIV84). The term *"seasons"* denotes change.

In the midst of the inevitability of change, God is our one constant. Centuries ago, the psalmist wrote, *"You are righteous, LORD, and your laws are right.... Your promises have been thoroughly tested, and your servant loves them"* (Psalm 119:137, 140). The author of the psalm said, in effect, "I've tested God's promises. Time has tested them. And they are still standing." Another psalm states, "*Your kingdom is an everlasting kingdom, and your dominion endures through all generations. The LORD is faithful to all his promises and loving toward all he has made*" (Psalm 145:13 NIV84). Our Creator made us, and He is faithful to all His promises. No matter what changes may come your way, you can depend on Him to fulfill what He has promised. If you are meant to have something because God promised it, you will have it as you receive it in faith and trust in Him to provide it.

The apostle Paul wrote, "*For no matter how many promises God has made, they are 'Yes' in Christ. And so through him the 'Amen' is spoken by us to the glory of God*" (2 Corinthians 1:20). Again, if God promised it, it's going to happen, regardless of what else occurs. No matter what other people predict about the future, if God has promised something, you can say, "Amen! It is done."

Thought: No matter what changes may come your way, you can depend on God to fulfill what He has promised.

Reading: Psalm 102:25–27

— DAY 74 —

THE TRANSFORMING POWER OF CHANGE

*"Be made new in the attitude of your minds; and...put on
the new self, created to be like God in true righteousness and
holiness."* —Ephesians 4:23–24

One reason that the things on earth aren't permanent is
because of God's creative nature. If you are a creative person, you're
always coming up with new things. That's the nature of God. He
is continually refining what He has created, as well as *"doing a
new thing"* (Isaiah 43:19). Some people like to think that they have
God figured out. They believe that because He doesn't change, He
won't do anything different from what they've already seen Him
do. When He brings or allows change in their lives in order to
further His purposes for them, they don't know how to react to
it. The change unsettles them because they didn't expect it. God
Himself doesn't change, but He's always working in our lives—and
His work involves transformation. Be assured that God is going to
allow something in your life to change.

If you read the Scriptures, you won't find any account of God
performing two miracles in exactly the same way. People often try
to make doctrines out of methods God has used in the past instead
of realizing that it is His nature, rather than His specific acts, that
is permanent. The *results* of those acts may be permanent, but His
actions will vary. Why? God is too creative to repeat Himself. His
creative nature promotes change. Unless we understand this, we
may constantly struggle against the changes He wants to promote
in our lives—changes intended to help us to grow and to fulfill the
reasons for our existence.

Let me put one note of caution here. This is not to say we should be apathetic and just accept everything that comes into our lives as God's will for us. Rather, we must learn to respond to changing circumstances, keeping in mind His ways and His purposes for us. This knowledge will enable us to deal with whatever changes come our way. We aren't guaranteed that our jobs will last, that our loved ones will always be with us in this life, and so forth. Thankfully, we know that we can rely on the unchangeable nature of God and His promises toward us in any critical changes we experience.

Thought: God Himself doesn't change, but He's always working in our lives—and His work involves transformation.

Reading: Hebrews 1:10–12

WHAT WILL YOU DO WITH CHANGE?

"We know that in all things God works for the good of those who love him, who have been called according to his purpose." —Romans 8:28

Since life involves a continual series of transitions, we should endeavor to be always prepared to respond to change rather than react to it.

If you react, you are a victim. If you respond, you are a victor.

If you react, change leads your life. If you respond, *you* lead change in your life.

The only defense against the negative impact of change is the anticipation of, and preparation for, its inevitability. The ability to respond rather than react puts you in control and reduces change to servanthood. Responding to change gives you the ability to use change for your benefit.

Brian Tracy, a best-selling author and speaker, said, "Resolve to be a master of change rather than a victim of change." Below are some positive ways you can respond to change in your life.

Overseeing change: Overseeing, or managing, change means that you have recognized and acknowledged change but are also taking some practical steps to address it. You are currently engaged in assessing how you can best control its impending impact on your life and vision.

Integrating yourself in change: Integrating yourself in change means that when change is happening to you, you become an active participator in its unfolding. This doesn't necessarily mean that you approve of it or support it. However, you understand that it is a reality, and you position yourself to move forward in life in the midst of it. You can remind yourself of these words of the apostle Paul: *"We know that in all things God works for the good of those who love him, who have been called according to his purpose"* (Romans 8:28).

Preparing and planning for change: This is one of the highest levels of response to the inevitability of change. Those who prepare and plan for change are never really surprised by it because they understand that change is integral to life. If you understand the nature of change, you always expect it. Therefore, the best "response" to changes that happen to you, around you, and within you is to anticipate them ahead of time, because you can prepare only for what you expect.

I have learned to avoid becoming unsettled, anxious, or angry about change by expecting it and always having a contingency plan. If there is nothing I can do about a certain situation, I put a plan into action to turn it to my advantage. This method can be used for both small inconveniences and critical events. This is the essence of *response to change*, as opposed to *reaction to change*, because it requires forethought. By planning and preparing for change, you can do the following:

+ Reduce anxiety, stress, and fear
+ Gain greater control over your circumstances and environment
+ Increase your confidence
+ Make change your servant

⌒

Thought: The only defense against the negative impact of change is the anticipation of, and preparation for, its inevitability.

Reading: Philippians 4:6–7

— DAY 76 —
CHANGE AND DECISION-MAKING

"A double minded man is unstable in all his ways."
—James 1:8 (KJV)

Many people's visions never take specific shape because they can't make up their minds what they want to do in life. The only decision they make is *not* to decide. Part of their indecision may be because they are afraid of introducing any type of change in their lives. Yet *prolonged indecisiveness is a vision-killer,* and it also drains the joy out of life. I've noticed that the most miserable people in the world are those who can never make a decision. The Bible expresses their situation well: *"A double minded man is unstable in all his ways"* (James 1:8 KJV). Indecisiveness carries over into all areas of life. A person who is indecisive is unsettled; he's on shaky ground. If you struggle with indecision, pray for God's wisdom, and then make a decision. (See James 1:5–8.)

Sometimes we know what we should be doing, but we're hesitant to take that first step. We always intend to do it, but we never do. Instead, we make excuses, such as "When my life gets less complicated," "When I feel more confident," or "After I pray about it more."

There is a story of two fishermen who were lost in a storm on a lake. The storm was blowing so fiercely that they couldn't see a thing. One of the fishermen said to his colleague, "We have two choices. We can pray or row. Which one should we do?" The other answered, "Let's do both!" That's the way you need to live. Instead of continually deliberating about what you need to do, just say, "Let's row." Even though you're scared, keep on rowing. Set a destination even while you're praying, and God will guide you where you need to go.

Another reason people aren't specific about their visions is that they're trying to do too much. Their problem isn't that they're hesitant about getting started, but that they're running around attempting too many things. Even though they are constantly constructing something, they're actually building nothing at all because they never complete anything.

I have learned this very important truth that has set me free from both indecision and ineffective busyness: *I was not born or created to do everything.* When we aim at everything, we usually hit nothing. Let me assure you: you were not born to meet all the needs on earth. Determine what you were born to do and then make decisions that will initiate the change needed to bring your vision to pass.

⌒

Thought: Prolonged indecisiveness is a vision-killer, and it also drains the joy out of life.

Reading: James 1:5–8

— DAY 77 —
CHANGE DRAWS OUT YOUR POTENTIAL

"I can do all things through Christ who strengthens me."
—Philippians 4:13 (NKJV)

When you experience change, you can rely on God's strength to enable you to flourish where you currently are in your life and to refine and expand your earlier goals. Let's look at several inter-related benefits of change that will help bring you closer to the fulfillment of your personal vision.

1. *Change draws out potential.* Potential is hidden, untapped power or dormant ability. Normally, ability remains dormant within a person unless they are highly moti-vated internally. People rarely decide on their own to release their true potential. The average person is not motivated enough to take the initiative to tap into their unused resources and capabilities but is satisfied with the status quo. Then, change comes and draws out their hidden potential. This is why change can be a real ben-efit to us. Change is vital because it is often the ignition that draws the power from the human battery.

2. *Change challenges potential.* Have you felt satisfied that you have accomplished something noteworthy—until a change takes place in your life or in your environ-ment that challenges you to go beyond your previous goals? We can become so enamored with what we have already completed that we cease to pursue what we can still accomplish. Change has a way of making us move beyond what used to impress us about ourselves. It

shortens our self-congratulatory celebrations and spurs us on to do something even greater.

3. *Change pressures potential.* Releasing one's potential usually requires the element of responsibility. Another way of saying this is that *ability* requires *responsibility* in order to be manifested. A change in conditions often forces us to accept duties and obligations that make us dig deeper into the reserves of our capacity.

4. *Change manifests the person behind the potential.* You don't know what you're carrying inside you until you have to deliver it. When an unanticipated event or situation occurs, it can prompt you to manifest a self that people didn't know was in you—that *you* never knew was in you. Unexpected change can help to manifest who you really are. When you challenge yourself to implement change in your life toward a better future, you reveal the true self within you.

Thought: Change is vital because it is often the ignition that draws the power from the human battery.

Reading: Psalm 18:28–30

— Day 78 —

GOD IS DOING "A NEW THING"

> *"See, I am doing a new thing! Now it springs up; do you not perceive it?"* —Isaiah 43:18–19

Our Creator knows that it is sometimes difficult for us to accept the changes He is making in our lives. He knows that we often expect things to remain the same and that we get used to His working in a certain way. So, He gave us some encouragement in the book of the prophet Isaiah: *"Forget the former things; do not dwell on the past. See, I am doing a new thing! Now it springs up; do you not perceive it?"* (Isaiah 43:18–19). "Seeing" refers to observing. Sometimes we don't recognize what's happening to us, around us, and in us. God says, "Open your eyes and study your environment. What do you perceive?"

Do you perceive the new things God is doing in your life? Stay in touch with Him through prayer and reading His Word so you won't become overwhelmed by change in your life. Stay close to Him, remembering that His character doesn't change. David, the poet-warrior-king, wrote, *"Therefore we will not fear, though the earth give way and the mountains fall into the heart of the sea"* (Psalm 46:2). How could he say that? Because he trusted in God as his *"strong tower"* (Psalm 61:3) and his *"rock"* (see, for example, Psalm 18:2, 46; 19:14).

Do you know your "Constant"? You must rely on the Unchangeable One in the midst of change to keep yourself stable and to keep your vision in focus during times of transition and upheaval. Seek to understand and interpret the changes in your life so that they don't shake you. Instead, use them to move forward in God's purposes for your life. You may even experience a time when there are so many changes that you begin to wonder, "Is God against me?" This is the time to reaffirm that He allows change to come in order to fulfill His purposes in us and through us. Reviewing and taking to heart these vital principles of change will help see you through:

+ Nothing is permanent except God and His promises.

+ God's character and nature are unchanging.

+ God uses change to advance His purposes in our lives.

Thought: Do you perceive the new things God is doing in your life?

Reading: James 1:16–17

— Day 79 —

GOD POSITIONS US IN LIFE

"The Lord will fulfill his purpose for me; your love, O Lord, endures forever—do not abandon the works of Your hands."
—Psalm 138:8 (niv84)

My wife and I once had a chance to visit Egypt. We toured the Sinai Desert, where we saw pyramids and were shown the long route people used to travel from Israel to Egypt. We learned that in the desert, flash floods sometimes occurred. They happened when it rained in the mountains, and the water ran down from the mountains and through the desert. Water would seemingly show up in the desert from nowhere. Yet the inhabitants of the desert used this change for their benefit by digging big pits to catch the water whenever it came. They would use the cisterns for their own drinking water and for watering their camels. These pits— whether full or empty—were all over the desert.

This was probably the kind of pit Joseph's brothers threw him into. The important point is that it was the right pit. The cistern was right next to the road that went from Israel to Egypt. It "just so happened" that a caravan came right alongside the pit on that particular road, giving Joseph's brothers the opportunity to sell him to merchants going to Egypt, making him a slave. Yet this seeming calamity was Joseph's free ride to his princely position!

Why does God position us in various places in life? God positions us to influence others, to change the course of events, and to protect His purposes. This is why I have been emphasizing the vital importance of discovering your purpose and vision in life, asking the question, *What were you born to do?*

Some of us get put into pits, but they're the right pits if our steps are ordered by the Lord. (See Psalm 37:23.) If Joseph had been in a different pit, those particular traders never would have purchased him, and he wouldn't have gotten to Egypt and become a ruler. As we wait in the pit for God to work, we must remember that there's a caravan on the way. This is how God works through change. Whether you're in the pit or the palace right now, the Lord is ordering your steps as you trust in Him.

Remember, Psalm 138:8 says, "*The LORD will fulfill his purpose for me.*" It continues, "*Your love, O LORD, endures forever—do not abandon the works of your hands.*" In other words, God will never abandon or cancel what He gave you birth to do. He is committed to it. That's how strong purpose is.

God will not abandon your purpose, but the question is, will *you* abandon it?

Are you committed to it?

You have to answer these questions for yourself. No outside force or circumstance can stop God's destiny for your life. Only you can stop it—by ignoring it, rebelling against it, or giving up on it entirely. God does not want you to miss what He's already guaranteed for you to accomplish.

⌒

Thought: God positions us to influence others, to change the course of events, and to protect His purposes.

Reading: Genesis 37:1–28

—Day 80—
YOU CAN'T RETIRE FROM CHANGE

"They will still bear fruit in old age, they will stay fresh and green." —Psalm 92:14

The greatest human temptation is to believe that you have arrived. We are all prone to move toward security, but security itself is an illusion. For example, consider the term *Social Security*. *Social* refers to society; *security* refers to permanence. However, this idea is impossible: society can never be permanent. Nothing in this life can be secured.

Because most people gravitate to the idea of security, they think that there's a place or a condition at which they can arrive in life where they can stop changing. This place or condition of security is often called "retirement." *Yet no one can "retire" from change. When you stop changing, you're through!*

I suggest that the older you grow, the more change you should initiate because change will keep you alive. It will enable you to be a contributing member of the human family. You can't wait for things to happen anymore. You have to *make* them happen. To do this, you have to work against the traditional perspective of our culture, which promotes the opposite. The older people grow, the less change they're encouraged to be involved in. People begin looking for security, stability—in essence, "tradition."

Yet eighty- and ninety-year-olds who are always active and traveling, visiting new places, are usually those who have sound minds and physical energy. Moreover, those who can't be physically active but have energetic spirits are always inspiring to be around. They're continually talking about experiences that animate them. They are the life of the party, no matter how old they are, because somehow they have learned the secret that change is to life what oxygen is to the body. It keeps giving you new, internal energy.

The goal in life is not to enshrine the history of our lives but to create additional history. The history that we read about in books and see in documentaries and dramas may be defined as "recorded change." We don't often record normal, everyday things. Instead, history is a record of people and events that have changed human life in some way. Therefore, if you want to leave a mark on history and not become lost in the machinery of tradition, you *must* initiate or maximize change.

We need to be people who are not afraid to explore the unknown and who plan for change instead of panicking when it comes. For you to become an effective responder to change, you must be willing to forget the effects of the previous change and reach for what is ahead. Remember that, in Philippians 3:10, Paul didn't say we were to *maintain what currently is* but to *reach forward to what is ahead*. We need to be proactive, progressive, and pro-responsive. In this way, we will become the designers of change and not the victims of it.

⌒

Thought: The goal in life is not to enshrine the history of our lives but to create additional history.

Reading: Psalm 92:12–15

— DAY 81 —
PREOCCUPIED WITH THE PAST?

"The former things will not be remembered, nor will they come to mind." —Isaiah 65:17

After earning my bachelor's and master's degrees in the United States, I returned to the Bahamas in 1980 with a vision for creating Bahamas Faith Ministries International (BFMI) and developing Third World leaders. As I moved forward with my plans, I encountered resistance and misunderstanding because I was attempting something unheard of at the time. What I was doing was not traditional for a Bahamian. I was leading change by creating a new "product" in an environment that wasn't used to it.

The forces of change that I initiated resulted in the creation of an organization headquartered on a small island that now reaches nations around the globe. The tides of change transformed my life as well as the lives of hundreds of thousands who have been educated and inspired through the organization's conferences and through my radio, television, and Internet programs; books; and international speaking engagements.

The apostle Paul wrote:

> I press on, that I may lay hold of that for which Christ Jesus has also laid hold of me. Brethren, I do not count myself to have apprehended; but one thing I do, forgetting those things which are behind and reaching forward to those things which are ahead, I press toward the goal for the prize of the upward call of God in Christ Jesus. (Philippians 3:12–14 NKJV)

If I had been preoccupied with the past, I never would have started BFMI or my work with Third World leaders. In fact, I probably never would have sought to go to college or to realize my God-given vision. Those who are caught up in the past and who merely accept the status quo will be led by change, not the other way around. Yet anyone who leads change will contribute significantly to their generation.

One way that we define greatness is by the amount of positive change a person has created. What would the world be like without the influences of the patriarchs Abraham and Moses, of the monarchs David and Solomon, or of the early church leaders? What would America have become without the influences of George Washington and Abraham Lincoln? What would the second half of the twentieth century have been like without Martin Luther King Jr., Nelson Mandela, and Ronald Reagan? These were people who were, in a sense, revolutionaries. They forged new frontiers.

And, of course, the One who has influenced the world the most is Jesus Christ. The amount of positive change He has initiated can never be calculated.

People who can forge new frontiers—whether on a large or a small scale—will be successful through change. The key to future *failure*, therefore, is to be preoccupied with the past and to cling to traditional ways of doing things. The key to future *success* is to respond like Paul: *"reaching forward to those things which are ahead."*

⌒

Thought: One way that we define greatness is by the amount of positive change a person has created.

Reading: Isaiah 65:17–18

— Day 82 —

MATURITY IS MEASURED BY RESPONSE TO CHANGE

"All of us, then, who are mature should take such a view of things."   —Philippians 3:15

Your level of maturity is measured by how well you handle change. Yesterday, we looked at Paul's statement in Philippians 3:13–14: *"One thing I do, forgetting those things which are behind and reaching forward to those things which are ahead, I press toward the goal for the prize of the upward call of God in Christ Jesus"* (NKJV). Paul was saying, in effect, "If you can forget what you did before, and press toward something you haven't done yet, that's maturity."

Who is able to do this in the midst of life's changes and difficulties? Our answer comes in Paul's next statement: *"All of us, then, who are mature should take such a view of things. And if on some point you think differently, that too God will make clear to you"* (Philippians 3:15).

Only mature people can stop living in the past and accept the approaching future. Consider carefully how I am using the word *maturity* here. It refers to responding constructively, no matter what hardships and challenges we face in life, instead of merely reacting and thereby causing ourselves further disappointment, pain, and lost potential.

Paul was certainly not saying—and neither am I—that it is immature to feel sorrow or to grieve when we experience tragedy and loss. Paul knew sorrow, and so did Jesus. Maturity, therefore, is measured by your capacity to *let go* or to "forget" the past and to *build* and *create* the future. Some people mourn for years over what happened, what didn't happen, what could have happened, what

171

they used to do, and how things used to be. Maturity is measured by one's capacity to respond effectively to the unexpected. Those who are mature look to the future and focus on fulfilling their purposes for living.

Since the maturity of your belief system will be tested by change, here are some principles to remember:

+ Change comes to test who we are and who we claim to be.

+ Our maturity is measured by our response to change.

+ Change will always manifest our maturity if it's truly there.

+ Change is a means by which we can *learn* the mature response to unsettling times.

⌣

Thought: Only mature people can stop living in the past and accept the approaching future.

Reading: Ephesians 4:11–15

— DAY 83 —
BE A WORLD CHANGER

*"These who have turned the world upside down have come
here too."* —Acts 17:6 (NKJV)

Initiating change is the highest level of response to change. When
you initiate change, you are responding to change by realizing its
potential and power and by actively creating it to further your
vision and goals for your life based on your purpose.

To initiate change means the following:

1. You determine what changes in your life and environment will best serve the purposes you have been called
   to fulfill on this earth.

2. You order your life and environment according to these
   best interests. In other words, your unique assignment
   and vision from the Creator produces the incentive to
   create the conditions and to gather the resources that
   will produce the changes necessary to fulfill His will for
   your life.

Proactive people are the ones who usually succeed in life—
against all odds. I refer to these men and women as "world chang-
ers." I challenge you to become a world changer, someone who initiates change, who makes things happen to fulfill your purpose
and who contributes your particular gifts to your generation.
Consider again Mother Teresa and the work she did among the
sick and poor in Calcutta. She stepped into her vision of helping
the "poorest of the poor" that God had placed in her heart.

In her lifetime, Mother Teresa encouraged others not to wait
for well-known leaders to do a job but to follow their own visions

and initiate the change that was needed. By acting when there was a real need and doing what she personally could do to help, Mother Teresa became a world changer. She influenced numerous others to awaken their own visionary gifts and, in doing so, multiplied her effectiveness thousands of times over.

There are people who say, "I'm open to change as long as it doesn't affect me, as long as it doesn't cost me anything." But all change will cost something, even if it's just the loss of the familiar. We must be willing to let go of what *isn't* working for us in order to pursue what is best for us.

Are you willing to let go of the past and become proactive about the future? If so, you are ready to become a world changer.

⌒

Thought: Proactive people are the ones who usually succeed in life—against all odds.

Reading: Acts 17:1–9

— Day 84 —

"I HAVE CONSIDERED MY WAYS"

"I have considered my ways and have turned my steps to your statutes." —Psalm 119:59

We each need to take a close look at where we are in relation to the purposeful changes we want to make in our lives. It's time to ask ourselves, "Am I on course, or have I taken a detour?" Most of us know the courses we are on. We know our daily habits. In our hearts, we know exactly what we're doing and where we're headed. But are we being honest about it with ourselves?

Sometimes, we may take a detour from our visions by experiencing a major crisis in life or by having a disastrous personal failing. I want to encourage you that even if you have stumbled or fallen, you can still make it to your destination. If you have had a personal failing, you will need to ask God for forgiveness and seek reconciliation with those whom you've hurt. Working through such detours means you must take a revised route in order to get back to the main path—but you will get there. Every setback or failure can be transformed into a testimony. God will turn things around, and you will be able to grow from it and tell others how you developed faith and strength in the midst of it.

Proverbs 14:12 states, *"There is a way that appears to be right, but in the end it leads to death."* Perhaps the way you've been living seemed right at one time, or you wanted it to be right, but it's led to a collision or a dead end. Sometimes people think they can outsmart God. You can't get away with shortcuts—or substitutes. Trying to substitute something else for God's plan for your life is like trying to run your car on orange juice instead of fuel.

Psalm 119:59 says, "*I have considered my ways and have turned my steps to your statutes.*" The writer of the psalm was saying, in essence, "I've thought about the way my life was going, and therefore I have changed course." So take time to "consider your ways"— look at what you're actually doing and where your actions are leading you. If you are off course, make a course correction right away. "*I will hasten and not delay to obey your commands*" (verse 60). If you know where you want to end up, recalculate and turn in the right direction.

ACTION STEPS TO FULFILLING VISION

Here are some questions for "considering your ways":

+ Am I truly satisfied with the course I'm currently on?

+ Is the course I'm on enabling me to fulfill my purpose?

+ Have I been deterred or distracted from my vision? If so, what happened? What disrupted my life that has taken me off course for weeks, months, or years? After the disruption, what has *kept* me off course?

+ Does what I'm doing have eternal value?

Unless you address these questions, your life will remain the same. You'll keep doing things that cause you to diverge from the path to your purpose. Recommit to your vision and then keep your word to *yourself* that you will do what it takes to fulfill it.

⌇

Thought: "Consider your ways"—look at what you're actually doing and where your actions are leading you.

Reading: Psalm 119:57–64

— DAY 85 —

THE GENERATIONAL NATURE OF VISION

"Let this be written for a future generation, that a people not yet created may praise the LORD." —Psalm 102:18

Ecclesiastes 3:1 says, *"There is a time for everything, and a season for every activity under heaven."* Like the calendar year, our lives have four seasons, and those seasons must come to pass.

The first season is birth and dependency. All of us go through this season in which we must rely totally on outside help, particularly from our families, for survival. We need to be taught and trained in what is right and wrong and what is important in life.

The second season is one of independence, in which we capture what we were born to do. We no longer depend on other people to give us a vision for life or to help us survive. We focus in on our own goals. We depend primarily on God, yet we rely on the help of other people to provide the resources that will enable us to live out our dreams.

The third season is interdependence. In this stage, we have become so free in our visions that we can give our dreams to other people. We can now pass along our visions to the next generation.

The final season is death, where our lives become the nourishment for other people's dreams in the next generation. *If people can't receive life from the legacy you leave when you die, then you really didn't live effectively.* People should be able to flourish on the fruit of the vision you leave behind on earth. You should live so effectively that your life will be in the hearts and memories of those who could never forget you or what you did.

Truly great people don't need monuments because we will always remember them. It doesn't matter if we don't know where the graves of Joshua or Nehemiah are. They lived so well that we can't forget them. If you live properly, history will not be able to ignore that you lived. Vision gives us assignments that will impact the earth. We must be able to say we have changed the world in some way while we were here and that we have left a mark for those who will come after us. As I wrote earlier, we were born to do something in life that leaves nutrients for the seeds of the next generation to take root in and grow. I again encourage you to make the years you have on this earth count. Discover and pursue the vision God has placed in your heart! To help you to do this, in the final days of this devotional, we will review guidelines for discovering and developing your personal vision plan.

⌒

Thought: People should be able to flourish on the fruit of the vision you leave behind on earth.

Reading: Psalm 102:18–28

—DAY 86—
EIGHT STEPS TO WRITING YOUR VISION

"Commit to the LORD whatever you do, and he will establish your plans." —Proverbs 16:3

Throughout *Vision with Purpose and Power*, we have seen that discovering and implementing your personal vision is a process of learning about yourself, growing in your relationship with and knowledge of the Lord, and continually fine-tuning your understanding of the vision God has given you. Therefore, as I emphasized earlier, when you first write your vision, realize that it won't be a finished product. You will keep refining it as God makes your purpose clearer as the months and years go by and as you experience spiritual and personal growth. In fact, it would be a good idea to review your personal vision on a regular basis. At least every six months to a year, set aside a block of time to pray about and reevaluate where you are in relation to your vision. You will add or take away certain elements of your plan as God refines your understanding of His purpose for you. Eventually, you will begin to see, "This is the real thing!"

Remember, if you never develop a life blueprint, God will have nothing to direct you in. My prayer is that you will stop the construction of your life right where it is and go back and draw solid blueprints that will lead you where you want to go in life through the vision God has put in your heart. Use the guidelines in these final devotions to begin or refine your life blueprint.

STEP ONE: ELIMINATE DISTRACTIONS

Sit down somewhere by yourself, away from any distractions and responsibilities, and allow yourself some uninterrupted time to think about your purpose and vision. Do this as often as you need to as you develop your plan.

STEP TWO: FIND YOUR TRUE SELF

Until you know who you are, why God created you, and why you're here, life will simply be a confusing experiment. Answering the following questions will help give you clarity and confidence regarding your personal identity.

+ Who am I?

+ Who am I in relation to God?

+ Where do I come from as a person?

+ How have I been created like my Source? (See Genesis 1:26–28.)

+ Why am I here?

Next, write out your personal purpose statement. Ask yourself, "What is my reason for existence as a human being and as an individual?" (You may want to write an answer now and then compare it with what you think after you have gone through the rest of the steps.)

⌣

Thought: Discovering and implementing your personal vision is a process of learning about yourself, growing in your relationship with and knowledge of the Lord, and continually fine-tuning your understanding of the vision God has given you.

Reading: Matthew 11:27–30

— DAY 87 —

IDENTIFY AND REFINE YOUR VISION

"Each of you should use whatever gift you have received to serve others, as faithful stewards of God's grace in its various forms." —1 Peter 4:10

True vision is the product of a clear sense of purpose and deep inspiration. The following questions will help you to identify and refine your personal vision. You'll be amazed at the way God will begin to open your mind to His purpose and vision for you. You'll begin to see things that you've never seen before.

STEP THREE: FIND YOUR TRUE VISION

Write down the answers to the following questions, read them over, think about them, pray about them, and begin to formulate ideas about what you want out of life.

+ What do I want to do with my life?

+ What would I like to do more than anything else, even if I was never paid for it?

+ What do I love to do so much that I forget to eat or sleep?

+ What am I inspired to do?

+ What is my deepest desire? What do I feel truly passionate about?

+ What is the idea that never leaves me? What are my constant, recurring dreams?

+ What do I continually imagine about my future?

+ What one thing would I do if I knew I could not fail at it?

+ What would bring me the greatest fulfillment?

+ Where do I want to be one year, five years, ten years, twenty years, thirty years from now?

Allow yourself to think freely. Don't put any limitations of time or money on your vision. Because many of us are influenced by others' opinions of us and by our own false expectations for ourselves, it may take you a little time to discover what you really want. Persevere through the process and dig down deep to find your true desires. Below is an activity to help you do this.

WRITE YOUR OWN LEGACY:

What would you like your eulogy to say about you? What would you like to be known for? What do you want to leave to this generation as a contribution? What would you want others (family members, colleagues, teachers, employers, neighbors) to say about you?

+ Family: What kind of husband, wife, son, or daughter do you want to be remembered as?

+ Society: What kind of impact would you like to leave on your community?

+ World: In what way would you like the world to be different because you were here?

Thought: True vision is the product of a clear sense of purpose and deep inspiration.

Reading: 1 Peter 4:8–11

IDENTIFY YOUR MOTIVATION, PRINCIPLES, GOALS, AND OBJECTIVES

"[Jesus] answered, 'Love the Lord your God with all your heart and with all your soul and with all your strength and with all your mind'; and, 'Love your neighbor as yourself.'"
—Luke 10:27

A vision from God is never selfish. It will always help or uplift others in some way. It is designed to make the lives of humankind better and to improve society. It inspires and builds up others. In Step Four, consider your true reasons for pursuing your vision.

STEP FOUR: DISCOVER YOUR TRUE MOTIVATION

Ask yourself the following:

+ What is my motivation for my vision?

+ Why do I want to do what I want to do?

+ How does my vision help others?

+ Can I accomplish my vision and still have integrity?

STEP FIVE: IDENTIFY YOUR PRINCIPLES

Next, identify your principles. Your principles are your philosophy of life. In other words, they are how you intend to conduct yourself. You must clarify what you will and won't do. These principles are your guides for living, doing business, relating to other people, and relating to life. You must settle them in your heart and mind so that you will have standards to live by.

The Ten Commandments are great principles and a good starting point for developing your own guiding principles. For example, you could write, "On my way to my vision, I will not steal, lie, or bear false witness. I won't worship any god but God the Father. I will not commit adultery. I will not covet," and so on.

+ Write out your life principles.

STEP SIX: CHOOSE YOUR GOALS AND OBJECTIVES

Goals are the steps necessary to fulfill your vision. What practical things do you need to do to accomplish your dream? Goals are clear markers that will take you where you need to go.

+ Write out your goals. (See the Personal Goal-Setting Program at the back of this book.)

Objectives are the detailed steps of your goals. They determine when you want things to happen. You must clearly delineate what you need to do and when you need to do it in order to get to where you want to go. For example, if you want to open a mechanics shop, and one of your goals is to go to school to learn mechanics, some of your objectives will be to choose a school, fill out an application, and start classes. Objectives should include specific timetables to keep you on target.

+ Write out your objectives.

⁓

Thought: A true vision is designed to make the lives of humankind better and to improve society.

Reading: Exodus 20:1–17

— Day 89 —

IDENTIFY YOUR RESOURCES

"But seek first his kingdom and his righteousness, and all these things will be given to you as well." —Matthew 6:33

To complete your vision plan, you must identify all the resources you will need to accomplish your dream.

STEP SEVEN: IDENTIFY YOUR RESOURCES

Identify your human needs:

+ What help do you need from others to fulfill your vision?

+ What kind of personal associations do you need to have—and not have?

Identify your resource needs:

+ What kinds of resources do you need to fulfill your vision? Don't worry about how large they may seem. Write them down.

Write down your strengths:

+ What are your gifts? What do you know you are good at?

Record all your answers and then make plans to refine your strengths. For example, if your vision requires that you will need to speak before large groups of people, you have to start stepping out and speaking to groups. You're probably going to be scared at first, yet God will give you opportunities to speak at different stages so you can develop your gift. You don't even know what you can do until you have to. Remember, people manifest some amazing gifts when they are under pressure!

Write down your weaknesses:

+ What does your vision need that you aren't good at?

Don't be ashamed of your weaknesses because everyone has something they are not good at. You don't have the monopoly on that. However, you must identify these areas because God will supply people to do what you cannot do toward your vision. You need other people in your life because your vision cannot be fulfilled by you alone. God may also have you attend seminars or classes to glean the knowledge or skill you may be missing at this point. Don't be afraid to learn new things. God will accomplish great plans through you!

Additionally, you can receive wise counsel from those who have walked before you and who have a vision that is close to your own. They will be aware of resource needs that you might not recognize this early in your plans. As the Scriptures say, *"Plans fail for lack of counsel, but with many advisers they succeed"* (Proverbs 15:22). Discuss the following questions with a few trusted mentors or leaders, and follow through for the success of your plans:

+ What do I want to accomplish?
+ What resources do I already have?
+ Who and what do I need to help me?
+ Where can I go for more information?
+ What do I need to read?
+ Who should I associate with?
+ How long should my vision take to complete?
+ How much will it cost?
+ What courses should I take?
+ Where can I gain experience?

Thought: Make plans to refine your strengths and address your weaknesses.

Reading: Matthew 7:7–11

— DAY 90 —

COMMIT TO YOUR VISION

"Commit your way to the LORD, trust also in Him."
—Psalm 37:5 (NKJV, NASB)

Once you have answered the questions and completed the exercises from the previous days—considering all aspects of your vision—it's time to do two final exercises before moving to step eight. These exercises are summaries of what you now understand about yourself, your purpose, and your vision. The first exercise is to formulate your personal mission statement. A written mission statement defines the purpose and reason for your existence (personal and corporate). It is a general statement of purpose that declares the overall idea of what you want to accomplish. It is philosophical and abstract rather than practical and concrete.

To help you write your personal mission statement, ask yourself the following questions:

1. What represents the deepest and best within me?
2. What would fulfill my gifts and express my capacity to contribute to humanity?
3. What integrates all my physical, mental, social, and spiritual needs?
4. What creates and reflects my principle-based values?
5. What would fulfill all my roles in life—family, professional, community, and generational?

+ Write your personal mission statement.

After you have written your mission statement, summarize your vision *in just one sentence.* This is a specific and concise statement of what you want to do in life. It should be something that will motivate you and keep you moving toward your dream. After you write it, place it where you can see it every day.

+ Summarize your vision in just one sentence.

STEP EIGHT: COMMIT TO YOUR VISION

You will never fulfill your vision if you are not committed to it. This is why the final step is to commit to pursuing it. You will need to make a specific decision that you are going to follow through with what you want to do, acknowledging that God may refine your plans as He leads you through the process. Also, you must commit your vision to God on a regular basis. Remember that Proverbs 16:3 says, *"Commit to the LORD whatever you do, and he will establish your plans."*

+ Commit to your vision.

+ Commit your vision to God.

As you move forward to implement your vision plan, remember these seven principles of vision, which are drawn from Habakkuk 2:2–3:

> Then the LORD replied: *"Write down the revelation and make it plain on tablets so that a herald may run with it. For the revelation awaits an appointed time; it speaks of the end and will not prove false. Though it linger, wait for it; it will certainly come and will not delay."*

1. The principle of documentation (write the vision)

2. The principle of simplification (make it plain)

3. The principle of shared vision (give it to the heralds)

4. The principle of participation (let them run with it)

5. The principle of timing (an appointed time)

6. The principle of patience (wait for it)

7. The principle of faith (it will certainly come)

~~~

Thought: You will need to make a specific decision that you are going to follow through with what you want to do, acknowledging that God may refine your plans as He leads you through the process.

Reading: Psalm 32:8

PERSONAL GOAL-SETTING PROGRAM

Year: _____

Name: _____

By God's grace, I commit to accomplishing the following goals this year:

PERSONAL SPIRITUAL GOALS

1. _____
2. _____
3. _____

PERSONAL FAMILY GOALS

1. _____
2. _____
3. _____

PERSONAL HEALTH GOALS

1. _____
2. _____
3. _____

PERSONAL ACADEMIC GOALS

1. _____
2. _____
3. _____

PERSONAL CAREER GOALS

1. _____
2. _____
3. _____

PERSONAL RELATIONSHIP GOALS

1. _____
2. _____
3. _____

PERSONAL FINANCIAL GOALS

1. _____
2. _____
3. _____

PERSONAL INVESTMENT GOALS

1. _____
2. _____
3. _____

SAMPLE GOALS:

- read seven books on spiritual subjects
- increase communication with family
- meet five new friends
- lose weight
- get a physical checkup
- take continuing education courses
- earn a master's degree
- open a savings account
- reduce or eliminate financial debt
- purchase real estate

ABOUT THE AUTHOR

Dr. Myles Munroe (1954–2014) was an international motivational speaker, best-selling author, educator, leadership mentor, and consultant for government and business. Traveling extensively throughout the world, Dr. Munroe addressed critical issues affecting the full range of human, social, and spiritual development. He was a popular author of more than forty books, including *The Principles and Power of Vision*, *The Principles and Benefits of Change*, *The Power of Character in Leadership*, *The Spirit of Leadership*, *Understanding the Purpose and Power of Prayer*, *A Woman of Purpose and Power*, and *A Man of Purpose and Power*.

Dr. Munroe was founder and president of Bahamas Faith Ministries International (BFMI), a multidimensional organization headquartered in Nassau, Bahamas. He was chief executive officer and chairman of the board of the International Third World Leaders Association and president of the International Leadership Training Institute.

Dr. Munroe earned B.A. and M.A. degrees from Oral Roberts University and the University of Tulsa, and was awarded a number of honorary doctoral degrees. The parents of two adult children, Charisa and Chairo (Myles Jr.), Dr. Munroe and his wife, Ruth, traveled as a team and were involved in teaching seminars together. Both were leaders who ministered with sensitive hearts and international vision. In November 2014, they were tragically killed in an airplane crash en route to an annual leadership conference sponsored by Bahamas Faith Ministries International. A statement from Dr. Munroe in his book *The Power of Character in Leadership* summarizes his own legacy: "Remember that character ensures the longevity of leadership, and men and women of principle will leave important legacies and be remembered by future generations."